PRINCETON STUDIES IN INTERNATIONAL FINANCE

No. 81, October 1996

CURRENT-ACCOUNT SUSTAINABILITY

GIAN MARIA MILESI-FERRETTI

AND

ASSAF RAZIN

INTERNATIONAL FINANCE SECTION

DEPARTMENT OF ECONOMICS
PRINCETON UNIVERSITY
PRINCETON, NEW JERSEY

PRINCETON STUDIES
IN INTERNATIONAL FINANCE

PRINCETON STUDIES IN INTERNATIONAL FINANCE are published by the International Finance Section of the Department of Economics of Princeton University. Although the Section sponsors the Studies, the authors are free to develop their topics as they wish. The Section welcomes the submission of manuscripts for publication in this and its other series. Please see the Notice to Contributors at the back of this Study.

The authors of this Study are Gian Maria Milesi-Ferretti and Assaf Razin. Dr. Milesi-Ferretti is an Economist in the Research De   l Monetary Fund and a Resear
Research. H
policy inclu
Tying Their
inflation and
Professor Ra
Public Econ
Associate of
and a Resea
Research. F
Consultant
Razin has
policy, mos
in the Wor
Chi-Wa Yu
publication

PRINCETON STUDIES IN INTERNATIONAL FINANCE

No. 81, October 1996

CURRENT-ACCOUNT SUSTAINABILITY

GIAN MARIA MILESI-FERRETTI

AND

ASSAF RAZIN

INTERNATION

DEPARTM

PRINCE

PRINCE

INTERNATIONAL FINANCE SECTION
EDITORIAL STAFF

Peter B. Kenen, *Director*
Margaret B. Riccardi, *Editor*
Lillian Spais, *Editorial Aide*
Lalitha H. Chandra, *Subscriptions and Orders*

Library of Congress Cataloging-in-Publication Data

Milesi-Ferretti, Gian Maria.
    Current-account sustainability / Gian Maria Milesi-Ferretti and Assaf Razin.
    p. cm. — (Princeton studies in international finance, ISSN 0081-8070 ; no. 81)
    Includes bibliographical references.
    ISBN 0-88165-253-9 (pbk.)
    1. Balance of payments—Mathematical models.   2. Debts, Public-Mathematical
models. 3. Fiscal policy—Mathematical models. I. Razin, Assaf.
II. Title. III. Series.
HG3882.M55 1995
382'.17—dc21   96-46436
                                                                                      CIP

Printed in the United States of America by Princeton University Printing Services at Princeton, New Jersey

International Standard Serial Number: 0081-8070
International Standard Book Number: 0-88165-253-9
Library of Congress Catalog Card Number: 96-46436

CONTENTS

FIGURES

TABLES

1 INTRODUCTION

When countries run large current-account deficits for a number of years, concerns often arise about the sustainability of those deficits. Should persistent current-account deficits above, say, 5 percent of gross domestic product (GDP) sound an alarm? Conventional wisdom says they should, especially when the deficit is financed with short-term debt or foreign-exchange reserves and when it reflects high consumption spending. It is worth asking, however, whether these, or any, thresholds on current-account deficits should be taken seriously, and worth determining which factors should be considered in evaluating whether sustained external imbalances are likely to lead to external crises. A cursory look at historical episodes suggests that a number of countries—Australia, Ireland, Israel, Malaysia, and South Korea, for example—have been able to sustain large current-account deficits for several years, but that others—such as Chile and Mexico—have not been able to do so and have suffered severe external crises.

The natural question that comes to mind in evaluating the viability of external imbalances is whether the country in question is solvent. Does it have the ability to generate sufficient trade surpluses in the future to repay existing debt? This notion of solvency, however, which is satisfied when the country meets its intertemporal budget constraint, may not always be appropriate in gauging such sustainability. There are two reasons for this. First, this concept considers only the ability to pay, not the willingness to pay. Although the present value of trade surpluses may theoretically be sufficient to repay the country's external debt, diverting output from domestic to external use so as to service the debt may not be politically feasible. Second, this notion often relies on the

We are grateful to Tamim Bayoumi, Eduardo Borensztein, Susan Collins, Enrica Detragiache, Rudiger Dornbusch, Stanley Fischer, Karen Lewis, Paul Masson, Enrique Mendoza, Peter Montiel, Michael Mussa, Jonathan Ostry, Dani Rodrik, Jorge Roldós, Julio Santaella, Miguel Savastano, and Lawrence Summers for useful discussions and suggestions, as well as to participants at the International Monetary Fund (IMF) conference on the Implications of International Capital Flows for Macroeconomic and Financial Policies, and seminar participants at the Federal Reserve Board, Princeton University, and Massachusetts Institute of Technology. We are also indebted to an anonymous referee for very constructive comments. The views expressed are those of the authors and do not necessarily reflect the views of the International Monetary Fund.

1

assumption that foreign investors are willing to lend to the country on current terms. This assumption may be unrealistic, especially when foreign investors are uncertain about the country's willingness to meet its debt obligations or its ability to do so in the face of an external shock. Clearly, the question of the availability of foreign funds, together with other market imperfections, imposes constraints on the sustainability of current-account imbalances that are additional to those imposed by pure intertemporal solvency.

This study argues that a notion of current-account sustainability that considers the willingness to pay and to lend, in addition to intertemporal solvency, provides a better framework for understanding the variety of experiences countries have had with protracted current-account imbalances. This more inclusive view draws on theoretical considerations to identify potential indicators of sustainability, then uses these indicators to interpret a number of country episodes characterized by protracted current-account imbalances (some of which ended with external crises). The nonstructural nature of the framework prevents us from quantitatively assessing the relative predictive power of these indicators. Our analysis suggests, however, that protracted current-account deficits are more likely to result in an external crisis when the size of the export sector is small, the real exchange rate is appreciated relative to historical averages, and the level of domestic savings is low. Weaknesses in the financial system are also found to be common to all the crisis episodes. Although external debt and interest payments do not clearly discriminate between crisis and noncrisis episodes when expressed as ratios of GDP, they do discriminate when expressed as ratios of exports. Whether the composition of external liabilities (short- and long-term debt, portfolio investment, and foreign direct investment) shows a consistent pattern across episodes is difficult to establish, given the limited number of episodes we consider and the large changes in the composition of capital inflows between the late 1970s–early 1980s and the 1990s (Calvo, Leiderman, and Reinhart, 1993, 1994, analyze determinants of capital inflows in the 1990s).

Why should we look at underlying "fundamentals" to measure sustainability, when financial-market perceptions of creditworthiness should be evident in price variables such as interest-rate spreads or quantity variables such as the size (and direction) of capital flows? The most obvious answer is that the financial markets may fail to signal sustainability problems until the problems are acute—the exchange-rate mechanism (ERM) crisis of 1992 and the Mexican crisis of 1994–95 are notable examples. Even disregarding the possibility of expectational

2

errors in financial markets, it is true that sudden shifts in market sentiment have been associated with the existence of expectations-driven multiple equilibria that give rise to the possibility of rational, self-fulfilling crises similar to bank runs. Such equilibrium outcomes can occur, however, only under certain conditions of vulnerability determined by the configuration of underlying fundamentals (Obstfeld, 1996); this constraint underscores the usefulness of looking at a broader set of indicators in evaluating sustainability. In addition, financial markets may be plagued by asymmetric information and problems of moral hazard, so that the behavior of borrowers and lenders is affected by the existence of explicit or implicit bailout guarantees. This implies that financial-market variables may fail to reflect fully the risks of external crisis.

Our study is organized as follows. Chapter 2 defines the notion of the sustainability of current-account imbalances. Chapter 3 develops the concept of intertemporal solvency, which uses simple relations derived from national-accounting identities to link current-account imbalances with intertemporal consumption and investment decisions. Chapter 4 examines the determinants of the willingness to pay and willingness to lend through a simple model of international portfolio allocation and moral hazard. Chapter 5 considers a set of potential indicators of sustainability, based on the theoretical analysis of the previous chapters, and Chapter 6 discusses the role of these factors in a few actual country experiences. Chapter 7 examines the performance of the indicators in singling out external crises. Chapter 8 concludes the study.

2 THE NOTION OF SUSTAINABILITY

The current-account deficit (or surplus) is the positive (negative) increment to the stock of the external liabilities of the economy; an evaluation of persistent current-account imbalances must consider their contribution to the buildup of this stock. Three related questions are frequently asked about an economy's external imbalances: Is a debtor country *solvent*? Are current-account imbalances *sustainable*? Is the current-account deficit *excessive*? We focus on the first two questions and briefly discuss the third.

Solvency and Sustainability

Solvency is defined theoretically in relation to an economy's present-value budget constraint. By this definition, an economy is solvent if the present discounted value (PDV) of future trade surpluses is equal to current external indebtedness. In the case of public finances, solvency implies that the present discounted value of future budget surpluses is equal to the current public debt. The practical applicability of this definition is inhibited by the fact that it relies on future events and policy decisions, without imposing any "structure" on them. In the case of fiscal imbalances, for example, virtually any deficit path can be consistent with intertemporal solvency if future surpluses are sufficiently large. Researchers have therefore attempted to define a baseline for future policy actions. In the case of public-sector solvency, this determination has typically been made by postulating a continuation into the indefinite future of the current policy stance in combination with no change in the relevant features of the macroeconomic environment (Corsetti and Roubini, 1991). This gives rise to the notion of "sustainability"—the current policy stance is sustainable if its continuation into the indefinite future does not violate solvency (budget) constraints.

Defining sustainability in relation to solvency is simpler for fiscal imbalances, because fiscal imbalances can be associated (at least to some degree) with direct policy decisions on taxation and government expenditure. Defining it in relation to solvency is more complex for current-account imbalances, because current-account imbalances reflect the interactions among the savings and investment decisions of the government and domestic private agents, as well as the lending decisions of foreign investors. Although government decisions may at first be taken as given, private-sector decisions may not. Furthermore, a key relative price, the exchange rate, is a forward-looking variable that depends, by definition, on the future evolution of policy variables.

An alternative way of asking whether current-account imbalances are sustainable is to determine whether a continuation of the current policy stance is going to require a "drastic" policy shift (such as a sudden tightening of monetary and fiscal policy, causing a large recession) or lead to a "crisis" (such as an exchange-rate collapse, resulting in an inability to service external obligations). If the answer is yes, the imbalance is unsustainable. Such a drastic change in policy or crisis situation may be triggered by a shock, either domestic or external, which causes a shift in the confidence of domestic and foreign investors and a reversal of international capital flows.[1] Note that the shift in the confidence of foreign investors may relate to their perception of a country's inability or unwillingness to meet its external obligations.

To give meaning to the definition of current-account sustainability, two issues must be addressed. First, if a continuation of current government policy into the indefinite future implies the violation of budget constraints, forward-looking private agents will anticipate that a "policy shift" has to occur. If external borrowing is growing without bound under the current policy, for example, the expectations of private agents will reflect the anticipation of a policy reversal, which could take the form of a debt default, a large devaluation, or a fiscal adjustment. Ignoring these expectations and their reflections on private-sector behavior (as is commonly the practice in baseline scenarios) can lead to forecasting errors and overestimation of the durability of such unsustainable policy. Private-sector anticipation of future policy changes is reflected, for example, in interest-rate differentials (when the exchange rate is pegged) and capital flight, both of which reflect expectations of a future devaluation or—for capital flight—of future taxation of domestic assets.

The second issue concerns the "trigger" that will give rise to the policy reversal. The evaluation of a policy scenario based on a model that incorporates the expectations of forward-looking private agents needs to specify the "event" that will provoke a policy shift. This event could be, for example, a given combination of a negative shock and a

---

[1] In the presence of uncertainty, the definitions of solvency and sustainability rely to some degree on expected values, implying that in some "states of nature," insolvency will occur. Under these circumstances, the issue is how likely it is that a "bad" scenario will occur and how vulnerable a country is to external shocks (which depends, among other things, on the expected distribution of the shock).

level of the ratio of external debt to GDP. The behavior of private agents and the implications of their behavior for the future path of the economy will depend on the particular trigger. The event that will provoke a policy shift is, in principle, different across countries and may reflect different degrees of vulnerability to external shocks or different capacities to undertake adjustment policies. An example of the first is the degree of diversification of the export base, which will affect the country's vulnerability to terms-of-trade shocks. An example of the second is the political economy situation, which will affect the government's ability to implement drastic changes in policy without causing social and political upheavals.[2]

"Excessive" Current-Account Imbalances

The question whether particular current-account balances are "excessive" can be answered only in the context of a model that yields predictions about the "equilibrium" path of external imbalances. Actual imbalances can then be compared to the theoretically predicted balances in order to judge whether they have been excessive or not. A benchmark for defining what constitutes an excessive deficit, for example, might be a representative-agent model with free capital mobility and investment-adjustment costs, in which consumption behavior would be based on the permanent-income hypothesis.

Two main strategies have been used for applying this model empirically. The first relies on a structural estimation of the model and concentrates on estimated responses to various kinds of shocks (permanent and transitory, country-specific and global; Leiderman and Razin, 1991; Glick and Rogoff, 1995; Razin, 1995). The estimated responses can be used to evaluate the persistence of current-account imbalances. The second strategy uses vector autoregression analysis to estimate the consumption-smoothing current account, which is equal to –PDV of expected changes in national cash flow, that is, output minus investment minus government spending (Sheffrin and Woo, 1990; Ghosh and

[2] The probability private agents attribute to a policy shift, which in a stochastic environment is state-contingent, may be taken as a measure of sustainability (Horne, 1991). A complementary notion of sustainability was put forward by Krugman (1985) in the context of the overvaluation of the dollar in the mid-1980s. Krugman extrapolated the future path of the exchange rate, using interest-rate parity, and predicted at this exchange rate the implied future path of the U.S. current-account balance. Having found an explosive path of U.S. external liabilities, he concluded that the level of the dollar (and its market-forecasted path) was unsustainable.

Ostry, 1995). The predicted optimal path of the current account is then used as a benchmark to determine whether actual current-account deficits have been excessive.

The concepts of solvency and sustainability are binary—a country is either solvent or insolvent, and a current-account deficit either sustainable or unsustainable—and imply an increasing order of restrictiveness. The concept of solvency, based on the intertemporal budget constraint, can accommodate a variety of future behavior patterns. The concept of sustainability, based on a continuation of the current policy stance, imposes a structure on future behavior. Within the notion of sustainability, we can also include cases in which a timely reversal of the current policy stance is sufficient to prevent a "hard landing."

The notion of excessive current-account deficits provides, instead, a quantitative metric based on deviations from an optimal benchmark (structurally derived from a model under the assumption of perfect capital mobility and efficient financial markets). This metric can be used as a basis for evaluating how close a given path of current-account imbalances is to unsustainability. One problem in using this metric as a basis for this determination, however, is that its benchmark relies on the absence of capital-market imperfections; deviations from the benchmark may therefore reflect simply the existence of liquidity constraints or other financial-market imperfections. In Chapter 3, we discuss the effect these imperfections may have on the supply of external funds, but we do not attempt to incorporate imperfect capital markets into an encompassing intertemporal model. We rely, instead, on the insights of the theoretical discussion and use a nonstructural approach to examine the sustainability of protracted current-account imbalances. Although we can thus incorporate a broader set of theoretical considerations than can be accommodated in a structural approach using state-of-the-art equilibrium models, we lose the ability to quantify our analysis.

3 EXTERNAL IMBALANCES AND INTERTEMPORAL SOLVENCY

We define intertemporal solvency as the circumstance in which the country as a whole and each economic unit within the country, including the government, obeys its respective intertemporal budget constraint. In the context of the resource constraint of the economy as a whole, the current account clearly plays a crucial role, because it measures the change in the net-foreign-asset position of the country. In an accounting framework, the current-account balance, CA, is defined as follows:

$$CA_t \equiv F_t - F_{t-1} = Y_t + rF_{t-1} - C_t - I_t - G_t$$
$$= S_{p\,t} + S_{gt} - I_t \,, \tag{1}$$

where F is the stock of net foreign assets, Y is GDP, r is the world interest rate (assumed, for simplicity, to be constant), C is private consumption, G is government current expenditure, I is total investment (private and public), S_p is private savings, and S_g is public savings. As the second equality in (1) shows, the current-account balance is also equal to the difference between national savings and domestic investment.

Following Sachs (1982), we calculate the annuity values of each form of income and spending, Y_t, C_t, G_t, and I_t, which we identify with the superscript P.[1] Government solvency requires equality between the

---

[1] The annuity value is calculated from the sum of present discounted values of the present and future flows and is given by

$$X^P = \frac{r}{1+r} \sum_{s=t}^{\infty} \left(\frac{1}{1+r} \right)^{s-t} X_s \qquad X = Y\,,\,C\,,\,G\,,\,I\,. \tag{2a}$$

To ensure solvency of the private sector, the present discounted value of lifetime consumption should be equal to the present discounted value of lifetime disposable income (private-sector wealth). Accordingly, the permanent (solvent) level of private consumption must equal the annuity value of private-sector wealth:

$$C^P = \frac{r}{1+r} \left[(1+r)F_{pt-1} + \sum_{s=t}^{\infty} \left(\frac{1}{1+r} \right)^{s-t} (Y_s - I_s - T_s) \right], \tag{2b}$$

where F_p is the private sector's level of net assets (domestic and foreign) and T is the tax burden. See Obstfeld and Rogoff (1996) for a more complete discussion.

permanent level of government consumption and the annuity value of public-sector wealth, which is given by the present discounted value of taxes plus the initial net-asset position of the government:

$$G^P = \frac{r}{1+r}\left[(1+r)F_{gt-1} + \sum_{s=t}^{\infty}\left(\frac{1}{1+r}\right)^{s-t}T_s\right], \qquad (2)$$

where F_g is the public sector's level of net assets. The net foreign-asset position of the country (F) is given by $F_p + F_g$, because government net liabilities vis-à-vis the private sector cancel out. Using (2) and (2b) together with the economy's resource constraint (1), we obtain the following expression for the current account:

$$CA_t = (Y_t - Y_t^p) - (C_t - C_t^p) - (I_t - I_t^p) - (G_t - G_t^p). \qquad (3)$$

Current-account imbalances in an intertemporally solvent economy thus reflect deviations of output, consumption, investment, and government spending from their "permanent" levels. To evaluate the effects on the current-account balance of deviations of, say, government spending, from its permanent level, we need a model that specifies the behavior of consumption, investment, and output. If private agents fully smooth their consumption path, private consumption (C_t) will be equal to C^P. Assuming that investment decisions are driven by technology and world real interest rates and that the capital stock and labor force are fully utilized in production, a positive deviation of government spending (G_t) from its permanent level (G^P) will generate a current-account deficit. This deficit is the result of the decisions of private agents to smooth consumption by borrowing from abroad during periods of temporarily high government spending. If, instead, output is above its permanent level, consumption smoothing will imply a current-account surplus. In a Keynesian setting, however, focusing on deviations between actual and potential output, positive deviations of output from its potential level are associated with current-account deficits.

An Operational Condition for Solvency

The solvency condition (external debt no higher than the present discounted value of future trade surpluses) is clearly of limited operational use, because it relies on the evolution of macroeconomic variables into the indefinite future without imposing any "structure" on the path of these variables. One can, however, derive a simple sufficient condition for solvency under the assumption that macroeconomic aggregates

9

are constant as a fraction of GDP, and that the interest rate and the rate of change of the real exchange rate are constant.

Assume that the domestic economy grows at a given rate (γ) that is below r.[2] Let s_t, p_t, p_t^*, and i_t^* be the nominal exchange rate, the domestic GDP deflator, the foreign GDP deflator, and the world nominal interest rate, respectively, and define the real exchange rate (q_t) as $p_t/s_t p_t^*$. We can then rewrite the current-account identity (1) as

$$s_t p_t^* F_t - s_t p_{t-1}^* F_{t-1} = p_t (Y_t - C_t - G_t - I_t) + i^* s_t p_{t-1}^* F_{t-1} , \qquad (4)$$

where F_t is now the stock of foreign assets denominated in foreign goods.[3] Let the ratio of foreign assets to output (f_t) be equal to $F_t/q_t Y_t$. Dividing both sides of (4) by nominal GDP ($p_t Y_t$) and rearranging terms, we obtain

$$f_t - f_{t-1} = tb_t + \frac{(1 + r) - (1 + \gamma_t)(1 + \varepsilon_t)}{(1 + \gamma_t)(1 + \varepsilon_t)} f_{t-1} , \qquad (5)$$

where tb is the trade balance, and ε is the rate of real appreciation of the domestic currency. This expression simply says that changes in the ratio of foreign assets to GDP are driven by both trade imbalances and a "debt-dynamics" term that is positively related to the world real rate of interest and negatively related to the rate of real-exchange-rate appreciation and the rate of domestic economic growth.

Consider now an economy in steady state, in which consumption, investment, public expenditure, and the stock of foreign assets (liabilities) are constant as a fraction of GDP. What is the long-term net resource transfer (trade surplus) that an indebted country must undertake in order to keep the ratio of debt to output constant? From equation (5), we obtain

$$tb = 1 - i - c - g = -\frac{(1 + r) - (1 + \varepsilon)(1 + \gamma)}{(1 + \varepsilon)(1 + \gamma)} f , \qquad (6)$$

where tb is the long-term trade balance. This expression highlights the role played by the average future value of world interest rates, domestic

---

[2] Otherwise a country could play "Ponzi games" indefinitely—that is, borrowing to repay interest on its outstanding debt, without violating solvency conditions, as long as total indebtedness rises at a rate that is below the economy's rate of growth. This possibility, which can arise in an overlapping-generations model of the Samuelson type (Gale, 1973), implies that the economy is following a dynamically inefficient growth path.

[3] Equation (4) shows that the ratio of current-account imbalances to domestic GDP is not invariant to the world inflation rate, just as the measure of the domestic budget

growth, and the long-term trend in the real exchange rate in determining the resource transfers necessary to keep the ratio of debt to GDP from increasing. Consider the case in which the long-term real exchange rate is constant ($\varepsilon = 0$). Condition (6) then suggests that the country's long-term absorption can be higher than its income only if the country is a net creditor. In this case, the country will run a trade deficit, equal to $f(r - \gamma)/(1 + \gamma)$, but a current-account surplus equal to $\gamma f/(1 + \gamma)$, thanks to the interest it earns on its foreign assets. Conversely, in the presence of economic growth, permanent current-account deficits can be consistent with solvency even when the growth rate is below the world interest rate, provided they are accompanied by sufficiently large trade surpluses.

Equation (6) has been used in practice as a rough solvency indicator. Cohen (1995), for example, considers the Mexican resource transfers (as a fraction of GDP) after the 1982 debt crisis as an "upper bound" on the feasible resource transfers for heavily indebted African countries and compares this magnitude with each implicit resource transfer from a high-debt country in terms of (6), in order to assess the country's solvency prospects (see also Cohen, 1992). This clearly necessitates inferences about the long-term behavior of ε, γ, and r. As for long-term movements in the real exchange rate, they reflect the evolution of the relative price of traded and nontraded goods within each country, as well as the changes in the relative price of traded goods across countries. According to the standard Balassa-Samuelson approach, the relative price of nontraded goods is driven by productivity differentials between the traded and nontraded goods in the domestic economy and the rest of the world. If we define d as the (logarithm of the) relative price of traded goods across countries, and a^T (a^N) as (the logarithm of) the productivity level in the traded (nontraded) sector, we can express the changes in the real exchange rate as follows (Frenkel, Razin, and Yuen, 1996, chap. 7):

$$\varepsilon = \dot{d} + (1 - \beta)\left[\frac{\upsilon}{\alpha}(\dot{a}_T - \dot{a}_T^*) - (\dot{a}_N - \dot{a}_N^*)\right], \qquad (7)$$

where a star indicates "foreign" variables, α (υ) is the labor share in the

---

deficit (inclusive of interest payments) is not invariant to domestic inflation. A more precise measure of the current account would need to correct for the fact that a portion of the measured current-account imbalances reflects anticipated repayment of principal in the presence of positive world inflation and foreign assets (liabilities) denominated in nominal terms.

traded- (nontraded-) goods sector, and β is the share of traded goods in the price index used for the calculation of the real exchange rate (the coefficients α, β, and υ are assumed for simplicity to be equal across countries). For given productivity in the nontraded-goods sectors, countries whose productivity increases in the traded-goods sector are more rapid than those of their trading partners will, *ceteris paribus*, experience an appreciation of the real exchange rate. Empirical evidence shows, however, that a significant proportion of the fluctuations in the real exchange rate is attributable to changes in the relative prices of traded goods across countries (the term d), rather than to differentials in productivity growth between the sectors producing traded and nontraded goods (Asea and Mendoza, 1994; Engel, 1993, 1996). This makes the assessment of long-term trends in real exchange rates difficult.

4 WILLINGNESS TO LEND AND WILLINGNESS TO PAY

So far, we have considered a world in which problems such as asymmetric information, moral hazard, and the absence of bankruptcy arrangements do not play a role in shaping international borrowing and lending. These problems, however, are particularly relevant for borrower countries characterized by shallow financial markets, by high vulnerability to terms-of-trade shocks, and by high political uncertainty. A vast literature, mostly spawned by the debt crisis of 1982, has used models of imperfect capital markets to study the way in which the equilibrium level of international lending depends on the form of creditor sanctions (including loss of reputation), the ability of the borrower to make credible commitments (for example, through investment), and the relative bargaining power among participants in debt renegotiations.[1]

The following framework emphasizes the factors that determine the willingness of international investors to lend to a given country and the interaction of those factors with others affecting the country's willingness to meet its external obligations.

Willingness to Lend: Portfolio Diversification

Consider a simple (static) model of international portfolio diversification with moral hazard. An international investor has to decide optimal portfolio allocation by choosing investment projects across $J + 1$ countries, indexed by j. The rate of return in the home country ($j = H$) expressed in foreign currency follows an independently and identically distributed (i.i.d.) stochastic process with mean ρ_H and variance σ_H^2. The remaining J countries (the rest of the world) are symmetric and have rates of return (r^j) that follow a random i.i.d. process with mean ρ and variance σ^2.

Assume that the international investor has a portfolio of size W, and denote by θ the share of the investor's portfolio allocated to the home country. The expected return on the portfolio is given by

[1] See Eaton and Gersovitz (1981) for an early analysis of sovereign borrowing in private financial markets, Eaton and Fernández (1995) for a recent theoretical survey on sovereign debt, and Cline (1995) for a retrospective on the debt crisis.

$$W[\theta\rho_H + (1 - \theta)\rho]$$

$$\rho_H = i_H - \frac{\dot{s}}{s} , \tag{8}$$

and the variance is given by

$$W^2\left[\theta^2\sigma_H^2 + \frac{(1 - \theta)^2}{J}\sigma^2\right], \tag{9}$$

where i_H is the rate of return in the home country's currency, s is the exchange rate between the home country and the rest of the world, and a dot indicates a time derivative. The variance on the rate of return (σ_H^2) represents the combined effect of exchange-rate risk and domestic interest-rate risk. Clearly, both ρ_H and σ_H^2 are endogenous, because they depend on the government's policy choices. This endogeneity is made explicit below (see equation (15)). The international investor is assumed to have constant absolute risk aversion, with a coefficient γ. Expected utility (U) is thus given by

$$U = W[\theta\rho_H + (1 - \theta)\rho] - \frac{\gamma W^2}{2}\left[\theta^2\sigma_H^2 + \frac{(1 - \theta)^2}{J}\sigma^2\right]. \tag{10}$$

Maximizing expected utility with respect to θ and denoting the foreign-currency value of home-country indebtedness (θW) by B_H, we obtain

$$B_H = \left(\sigma_H^2 + \frac{\sigma^2}{J}\right)^{-1}\left(\frac{i_H - \dot{s}/s - \rho}{\gamma} + W\frac{\sigma^2}{J}\right). \tag{11}$$

Figure 1 depicts the supply of external finance (B_H) as a function of the mean rate of return in the home country (ρ_H), which will be identified as the cost of foreign borrowing. From equation (11), we can verify that the supply schedule is upward-sloping; that is, the country has to raise the rate of interest (adjusted for expected exchange-rate changes) in order to elicit more capital from abroad. Furthermore, the supply schedule shifts upward as the opportunities for international diversification (J) rise (as in the case of "emerging markets"), as the country's credit and exchange-rate risk (σ_H^2) increases, and as the rate of interest in the rest of the world (ρ) increases. It shifts downward as the riskiness of the rest of the world's investment projects (σ) rises and as the size of the world's portfolio (W) increases.

14

FIGURE 1

SUPPLY OF EXTERNAL FUNDS

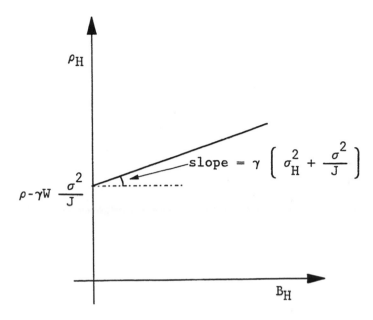

At the given level of external liabilities (B_H), a country must, in order to elicit external funding, pay the rate of interest (ρ_H) that is determined as the intersection between the supply-of-external-funds schedule and the vertical line originating at B_H. If a "bad" shock occurs, shifting the supply schedule upward, there will be an increase in the country's cost of external borrowing (ρ_H), and this increase may force the country to change its policy stance in order to generate the additional flow of resources necessary to service external liabilities.[2] In this context,

---

[2] Equation (11) can be rearranged to yield a risk-premium-adjusted interest-rate-parity condition as a function of the deviation of the home country's portfolio share (θ) from the minimum variance portfolio share (θ_{min}):

$$rp = i_H - \frac{\dot{s}}{s} - \rho = \gamma W(\sigma_H^2 + \sigma^2/J)(\theta - \theta_{min})$$

$$\theta_{min} = \frac{\sigma^2/J}{\sigma^2/J + \sigma_H^2} . \tag{11a}$$

The risk premium is exogenous in this model, and the home country's share of the world portfolio adjusts to ensure that (11) holds. A more complete model would endogenize the rate of return and its variance, the rate depreciation, and, hence, the risk premium. Dornbusch (1990) emphasizes the importance for international investors (or for domestic residents holding funds abroad) of the option value of waiting for determining the

15

Calvo (1995) shows how small "news" about the mean return of the investment project in the home country can have a large effect on the share of world portfolio allocated to that country when the portfolio is well diversified (J is large). In a similar context, Calvo and Mendoza (1996b) find that when it is costly for international investors to obtain information about country risk, investors' herding behavior can lead to several different equilibrium portfolio allocations. This implies that a sudden shift in investors' sentiment can lead to drastic changes in capital flows for a given country. Furthermore, the range of possible allocations widens when J increases.[3]

How would structural and policy factors impinge on the variables that determine the willingness to lend in the stylized portfolio model presented above? The domestic rate of return can be linked with the economy's prospects of growth in productivity and with fiscal policy (directly in the form of current tax rates, and indirectly through expected future taxation needed to repay the public debt). It will also be affected by the efficiency with which domestic financial markets intermediate foreign funds. The variance of domestic returns is linked, for example, to the overall degree of macroeconomic stability and, in particular, to the vulnerability of the domestic economy to shocks such as fluctuations in the terms of trade. In this context, the variance is reduced when the diversification of the production and export structure increases.

Willingness to Pay and Lend: The Role of Asymmetric Information

In the portfolio-diversification model, the upward-sloping supply of external funds was driven by the risk aversion of international investors. The existence of informational asymmetries between borrowers and lenders, which can be particularly pronounced in an international context, provides an additional reason for the less-than-perfect elasticity of supply of external funds. As shown in Stiglitz and Weiss (1981) in the context of bank lending, credit rationing can occur when borrowers are better informed than international investors are about the riskiness of projects (see Folkerts-Landau, 1985, for an open-economy application). The fundamental factor is that the rate of interest a bank charges

required risk premium for investing in the country.

[3] The multiplicity of equilibria stems from the fact that the cost and benefit (in terms of reduced variance) of obtaining new information depend on deviations of the individual portfolio choice from the world portfolio. In essence, the world portfolio represents an externality in the individual's utility-maximization problem.

may itself affect the riskiness of loans by either affecting the action of borrowers (the moral-hazard or incentive effect) or sorting potential borrowers (the adverse-selection effect). In addition, in the context of international sovereign lending, enforcement problems can exacerbate the effects of informational asymmetries. We illustrate the moral-hazard channel below.

Suppose that the country is risk neutral, and that it is charged an interest rate (r_H) if it borrows an amount (B) expressed in foreign currency. The country will have an incentive to default on its loan if the default costs (a fraction, $1 - \delta$, of the real return on its project, Y) plus the real collateral (C) are lower than the amount of repayment:

$$ C + (1 - \delta)Y < \frac{s}{p}B(1 + r_H) \,, \tag{12} $$

where p is the domestic price level, so that s/p is the real exchange rate. The collateral (C) can be interpreted as loan guarantees or as those assets that can be seized by the lender in the event of a default. The default costs $([1 - \delta]Y)$ could include the present value of the cost of penalties imposed on a defaulting country, such as trade disruptions and isolation from international capital markets, and an evaluation of the "reputation cost" associated with default.

A surprise real depreciation of the domestic currency (caused, for example, by a negative terms-of-trade shock) increases, *ceteris paribus*, the probability of default. Furthermore, investors' perception of the policy instruments the government will use to meet external obligations is influenced by political economy considerations. Capital flight driven by fear of direct taxation or exchange-rate depreciation, for example, can increase external debt (B) beyond the accumulated level of past current-account imbalances.[4]

The existence of implicit or explicit bailout clauses can exacerbate problems of moral hazard, yielding effects analogous to those of decline in collateral. The international financial community may be unwilling to let a country default on its debt obligations, because it wants either to protect foreign investors or to avoid the trade and capital-market disruptions that a default could induce. Moral-hazard problems may also be intensified by the implicit or explicit bailout clauses within a debtor country. Excessive borrowing by the banking sector, for example, can be

---

[4] In this case, B will represent gross external imbalances for the country as a whole. The virtual impossibility, however, of taxing foreign assets held abroad by domestic residents makes these imbalances the relevant measure of debt.

induced by expectations of a government bailout should the sector run into financial difficulties.

To illustrate the effect of moral-hazard problems on the supply of external funds, suppose that a country can choose between two investment projects, 1 and 2, and assume for simplicity that purchasing-power parity holds, so that $s/p = 1$. The expected return to the projects (i) is

$$\pi_i = E[\max(Y_i - (1 + r_H)B, (1 - \delta)Y_i - C)] \qquad i = 1, 2 . \quad (13)$$

The derivative of the expected return with respect to the rate of interest (r_H) is given by

$$\frac{d\pi_i}{dr_H} = -B\left(1 - F_i\left[\frac{(1 + r_H)B - C}{\delta}\right]\right), \qquad (14)$$

where F_i (.) is the probability that Y_i is less than $([1 + r_H]B - C)/\delta$ of default using the projects (i). If, for some r_H, $\pi_1 = \pi_2$, then an increase in r_H would lower the expected return from the project that had the higher probability of repaying the loan by more than the other project. The increase in the interest rate thus results in the country's preferring the project with the higher probability of default. An increase in world interest rates could also exacerbate problems of adverse selection within the domestic financial market (that is, a worsening in the average quality of borrowers), thus implying a less efficient allocation of resources by domestic financial institutions and a worsening of repayment prospects for foreign lenders.

The expected rate of return to the international investor and its variance will be given by

$$E(\rho_H) = (1 - F_i)r_H + F_i\frac{C + \delta Y_{iL}}{B}$$

$$\sigma_H^2 = F_i(1 - F_i)\left(r_H - \frac{C + \delta Y_{iL}}{B}\right)^2, \qquad (15)$$

where Y_{iL} is the expectation of Y_i, conditional on Y_i's being below the default cutoff level, $[(1 + r_H)B - C]/\delta$. Consider, first, the expected rate of return. By raising the interest rate (r_H), the probability of default (F_i) rises *for a given project*. Moreover, as a consequence of the interest-rate increase, the firm is more likely to choose a riskier project, thereby further increasing the probability of default. Even if the

18

foreign investor were risk neutral, he or she could find it optimal to "ration" credit supply at a given interest rate, rather than to raise the rate in the face of an excess demand for credit. This would happen if the expected return from the loan were actually to fall with an increase in r_H, as a consequence of the increase in the probability of default. The possibility of credit rationing is enhanced by the foreign investor's risk aversion. Indeed, credit rationing could occur even when the expected return (ρ_H) increases with r_H, because the variance of returns rises as well (equation 15).

For our purposes, we can consider (15) as establishing a positive relation between the mean rate of return (ρ_H) and its variance (σ_H^2). This implies that the credit-supply curve for the country will be even steeper than in Figure 1 (see also equation 11), and that it may entail credit rationing—that is, the foreign investor is unwilling to lend to the country more than a given amount at an interest rate at which the country would demand more funds.

The foregoing analysis underscores the possibility that external funds will "dry up" when an economy is hit by a negative shock of the kind described earlier. The trigger for a crisis could come from the foreign investors' perceptions of condition (12)—that is, from the likelihood that the debt burden $(B[1 + r_H])$ will exceed $C + \delta Y$. This can be caused by factors such as an increase in world interest rates, a negative supply shock such as a terms-of-trade decline, a change in the perceived solvency of the financial sector that would call for a government bailout, or a change in the perceived political costs of default. Thus, the preexisting policy can turn out to be unsustainable.

Moral-hazard problems in international borrowing and lending may also arise when the borrower can take "hidden actions" that affect output and, hence, the ability or willingness to meet external obligations. Gertler and Rogoff (1990) emphasize the way in which these problems may arise when a borrower cannot commit to using funds for investment, rather than for "disguised consumption" or capital flight. Their argument links the intensity of moral-hazard problems—and, thus, the level of lending—with the level of investment, or inversely, with capital flight; it also shows that foreign direct investment may be a way for foreign investors to ensure the "appropriate" final use of their funds.

What other macroeconomic and structural features of a borrower can affect the variables for willingness to pay and willingness to lend? In principle, variables that increase the cost of default on foreign obligations (by raising, for example, the impact on the domestic economy of

19

sanctions or isolation from international capital markets) strengthen the willingness to pay and therefore make a sudden reversal in capital flows less likely. If default is associated with trade disruptions, its cost will be higher for more open economies. If the "punishment" for default resides in the inability to borrow and lend on international capital markets (at least for some time), its cost will be higher for countries with higher output variability, because of the inability to smooth consumption.

5 INDICATORS OF SUSTAINABILITY

What should be considered when evaluating the sustainability of current-account deficits? In this chapter, we discuss several potential indicators, based on the analysis of solvency and the willingness to lend. We focus, in particular, on the country's economic structure, macroeconomic policy, and political economy. Some of these indicators are linked to the capital account, as well as to the fundamentals underlying the current account. We also consider the possibility that the type and size of external shocks are central to determining whether a country with large current-account imbalances will experience a crisis. We thus include indicators meant to capture the intensity of the shocks as well as a country's vulnerability to various types of external shocks.

It is important to distinguish between cases in which protracted current-account deficits are linked to severe domestic macroeconomic problems and those in which they are not so linked, but in which they may still reflect an external problem. In the first instance, the macroeconomic imbalances themselves would point to the "unsustainability" of the current policy stance and would therefore be an indicator of an impending domestic crisis, such as runaway inflation or public-sector insolvency. The crisis might also have an adverse external dimension, including (partial) default on external obligations. A policy reversal designed to address these domestic imbalances would in all likelihood also reduce external problems. Public-sector imbalances, for example, might drive a process of high inflation, as well as create problems of fiscal insolvency. In the presence of imperfect substitution between private and public savings, these imbalances could also be linked to large external imbalances. If a high degree of substitution between private and public savings exists, however, fiscal imbalances would indicate domestic problems, rather than a problem of current-account sustainability. When protracted current-account deficits are not linked to severe domestic macroeconomic imbalances, the evaluation of current-account sustainability is more complex, because there is no clear "policy reversal" needed to address a domestic problem (for example, the fiscal balance may be in surplus and inflation under control). We therefore examine a broad set of macroeconomic and structural indicators that economic theory suggests are important for assessing external sustainability and "match" them with several episodes of persistent current-account imbalances.

21

Structural Features

Savings and investment. The current-account balance is determined by the difference between national savings and domestic investment. For a given current-account balance, the *levels* of savings and investment can have implications for the sustainability of the external position. Because high levels of investment imply higher future growth through the buildup of a larger productive capacity, they enhance intertemporal solvency (equation 6). High savings and investment ratios can also signal creditworthiness to international investors, because they act as a form of commitment to higher future output and thus raise the perception that the country will be able to service and reduce external debt. In terms of equation (12), higher investment will be reflected in a higher present value of output (a higher Y), which will reduce default risk.

This argument assumes that investment is necessarily growth enhancing and that it strengthens the ability to repay external debt. Investment projects, however, may be chosen inefficiently, because of financial-market distortions or because they are driven by political priorities. Relative-price distortions, for example, may skew investment toward the nontraded-goods sector, therefore failing to enhance a country's ability to generate future trade surpluses. Under these circumstances, high levels of investment may not enhance sustainability.

Economic growth. Rapidly growing countries can sustain persistent current-account deficits without increasing their external indebtedness relative to GDP (see, for example, equations 5 and 6). We have emphasized the way in which the accumulation of physical capital through investment enhances a country's ability to service its external obligations; the same role is played by other engines of economic growth, such as the accumulation of human capital and increases in total factor productivity.

The sectoral composition of growth may be an additional indicator of potential external difficulties. In particular, low export growth can reflect an exchange-rate misalignment, which may point to the need for a policy reversal. A related argument is that, for a small open economy, large external trade may imply a more diversified input base for production and, hence, higher productivity growth. A positive impact on productivity can also come from access to technology embodied in internationally traded goods. Coe and Helpman (1995) and Coe, Helpman, and Hoffmaister (1994) provide evidence for the importance of international productivity spillovers.

Openness and trade. The degree of openness of an economy can be defined as its ratio of exports to GDP. In order to service and reduce external indebtedness, a country needs to rely on the production of traded goods as a source of foreign exchange. Clearly, countries that have large export sectors can service external debt more easily, because debt service will absorb a smaller fraction of their total export proceeds. If capital flows are interrupted, a country will need to shift resources toward the exports sector in order to generate the foreign exchange necessary to service external debt. Because this shift cannot occur instantly, sharp import compression may become necessary, and this may have adverse consequences for domestic industries relying on imported inputs (Sachs, 1985; Sachs and Warner, 1995). Import compression may be even more costly in a relatively closed economy, because it is more likely to entail cuts of "essential" imported inputs (Williamson, 1985).[1]

The size of the export sector can also be related to the willingness to lend and willingness to pay. Insofar as debt default is associated with trade disruptions, such as difficulties in obtaining export credits, it may be more costly for an open economy. The larger the size of the export sector, moreover, the larger will be the constituency against actions (such as debt default) that might entail trade disruptions. The theory of international borrowing sketched in Chapter 4 (see equation 12) suggests that higher costs of default will reduce the likelihood of sudden reversals of capital flows, because foreign investors will perceive the country as being less risky.

A more open economy is more vulnerable to external shocks, however, such as fluctuations in the terms of trade or reductions in foreign demand. This vulnerability is increased, and the ability of a country to sustain deficits weakened, if the country has a narrow export base or is particularly dependent on raw materials for its imports. It is reduced if the country's composition of trade is well diversified across commodities. Ghosh and Ostry (1994) find support for this view in the context of a model based on precautionary savings. Mendoza (1996) presents evidence for an association between the *volatility* of the terms of trade and lower economic growth.

Composition of external liabilities. The composition of external liabilities may affect the ability of a country to absorb a shock smoothly. This possibility has been widely discussed in the context of both the debt crisis (Cline, 1995) and the more recent phenomenon of large capital flows directed toward some developing countries (Calvo, Leiderman, and Reinhart, 1994; Fernández-Arias and Montiel, 1996). In general terms,

---

[1] In evaluating the relation between the size of the export sector and current-account sustainability, "exogenous" determinants of openness, such as the size of the economy, should also be taken into account.

23

we can distinguish between debt and equity, as well as between different debt and equity instruments. In principle, equity financing allows asset-price adjustments to absorb at least some of the negative shocks, so that part of the burden is borne by foreign equity investors. In the case of foreign-currency-debt financing, by contrast, the country bears most of the burden, provided it does not default. The structure of equity and debt liabilities is also important for evaluating a country's vulnerability to shocks. With regard to equity, it is often argued that portfolio investment is potentially more volatile than foreign direct investment.[2] With regard to debt, the maturity structure, currency composition, and interest structure (fixed or floating) of the debt will all affect a country's vulnerability to shocks. Short-term maturities, a bunching of debt redemption, foreign-currency denomination, and variable interest rates will enhance the risk of external shocks because they magnify the impact on the debt burden.

Financial structure. The links between a country's financial structure, its macroeconomic policy, and the likelihood of financial crisis have been intensively examined recently, following the resumption of large capital flows to developing countries in the early 1990s and the Mexican crisis of 1994–95 (Rojas-Suarez and Weisbrod, 1995; Goldstein, 1996; Kaminsky and Reinhart, 1996). In developing countries, financial intermediation is typically dominated by the banks; bank deposits are the most important form of private savings, and bank loans are the main source of finance for firms. Problems of asymmetric information are particularly important in less-developed financial systems. Because the disciplinary effect of competition with alternative forms of financial intermediation is limited, the role of bank supervision is essential. The fact that banks are more likely than other financial institutions to be bailed out by the central bank (government) can also imply more risk-taking behavior in such a bank-dominated financial system. Conflicts are likely to surface with respect to the central bank's supervisory role when the central bank is itself involved in direct lending, financed through high-reserve requirements. The quality of bank portfolios can

---

[2] Claessens, Dooley, and Warner (1995), however, find that in a sample of industrial and developing countries, the statistical labels "short-term" and "long-term" generally do not provide information regarding the persistence and volatility of flows. Razin, Sadka, and Yuen (1996) provide some theoretical underpinning for a ranking of different types of capital flows. Specifically, they argue that in the presence of asymmetric information between domestic and foreign suppliers of capital, there is a "pecking order" among types of capital flows, with foreign direct investment being preferable on efficiency grounds to portfolio debt, which in turn is preferable to portfolio equity.

also be affected by political influence on lending decisions, such as lending to state-owned enterprises.

As underscored by Goldstein (1996), the ability of the central bank to exercise its role as a lender of last resort is limited when the exchange-rate regime is not flexible. Under these circumstances, monetary policy is "tied to the mast" because of the need to defend the exchange-rate peg; the banking system will thus be more vulnerable to sudden reversals in capital flows.

Capital-account regime. When the capital account is very open, *de jure* or *de facto*, a country is more vulnerable to sudden reversals in the direction of capital flows. This reversal may concern domestic as well as foreign capital.[3] Clearly, the degree of *de facto* opening of the capital account is endogenous and depends, in particular, on the strength of the incentives to export capital (the risk-adjusted rate-of-return differentials caused by misalignments in domestic policy, political instability, and so forth). Capital controls are a distortion that puts a wedge between the rates of return on capital in the domestic economy and abroad. They can also affect the consistency of the macroeconomic policy stance by, for example, allowing a government temporarily to pursue an expansionary monetary policy while maintaining a fixed exchange rate—thereby weakening the current account and eventually causing the collapse of the peg.[4] The disciplining effect of an open capital account can prevent such inconsistency and can serve as a signal of a country's commitment to the pursuit of "sustainable" policies. Foreign investors will regard such a country as creditworthy, a perception that will contribute to reducing the cost of capital for that country and to increasing its supply of foreign funds (Bartolini and Drazen, 1996). Economic research and practical experience have also highlighted, however, the potential dangers of poor financial supervision and a weak banking system when associated with an open capital account (Diaz-Alejandro, 1985).

In sum, the openness of the capital-account itself is an ambiguous indicator of current-account sustainability. Although greater openness increases the exposure to adverse external shocks, it also provides a disciplining role on domestic policies.

[3] This is exemplified by the experience of several Latin American countries (Argentina, Mexico, Peru, and Venezuela) in the run-up to the debt crisis (Diaz-Alejandro, 1985; Sachs, 1985). For these countries, the level of "official" foreign debt at the time of the debt crisis was much higher than the cumulative value of past current-account imbalances, a level indicating that the accumulation of debt had financed not only an excess of imports over exports, but also outflows of private capital.

[4] Reverse causality is also possible. Countries with large current-account deficits may impose capital controls in order to stem reserve losses (Grilli and Milesi-Ferretti, 1995).

Macroeconomic Policy Stance

The degree of exchange-rate flexibility and exchange-rate policy. The degree of exchange-rate flexibility in response to external shocks can affect the ability of an economy to sustain current-account deficits. A rigid exchange-rate regime buffeted by external shocks may be the target of speculative attacks that precipitate an external crisis (Krugman, 1979; Flood and Garber, 1984). In such a context, the level of the real exchange rate is an important indicator of sustainability. A persistent appreciation in the real exchange rate can be driven by "fundamental" factors such as high productivity growth in the traded-goods sector, or favorable terms-of-trade shocks. In the context of a fixed or managed exchange-rate system, however, it could also reflect a fundamental inconsistency between the monetary-policy stance and the exchange-rate policy, thereby giving rise to "overvaluation." In this instance, the overvaluation would typically be maintained by high domestic interest rates and by the presence of capital controls and would encourage a decline in savings as domestic residents intertemporally substitute present for future consumption. It would also cause a decline in economic activity, both because high interest rates would be necessary to maintain the exchange-rate peg and because the traded-goods sector would be "priced out" of world markets. These effects would contribute to a widening of current-account imbalances and a loss of foreign-exchange reserves. The foreign-reserves drain might then be reinforced by expectations of a future devaluation. Finally, the weakening of the export sector would hinder the ability of the country to sustain external imbalances.

Large capital inflows could also cause an appreciation in the real exchange rate, although it would result in an overvaluation only to the extent that the capital flows were not driven by long-term fundamentals, but, rather, by factors such as a noncredible exchange-rate stabilization or an excess volatility of short-term flows (Calvo, 1986). Weaknesses in domestic financial intermediation and supervision (discussed below) can hinder the efficient allocation of capital inflows between consumption and investment and can contribute to the overvaluation.

It is difficult in practice, however, to make the definition of real-exchange-rate overvaluation operational in the absence of a well-established framework of real-exchange-rate behavior (Edwards, 1989). In developing countries that have undertaken structural reforms, large capital inflows and appreciation in the real exchange rate may reflect an increase in productivity and in the return to capital; if current-account deficits also emerge because of the underlying increase in

26

permanent income, it would not be an indicator of unsustainability. The difficulty lies in evaluating the degree to which a real appreciation reflects improved fundamentals.

Fiscal balance. To examine the relation between fiscal and external imbalances, we start from a benchmark "debt-neutrality" case in which there is no correlation between the public-sector deficit and current-account imbalances (Barro, 1974). This can be seen most easily in the context of the intertemporal framework of Chapter 3 (see equation 3): the current account is independent of the time profile of taxation and, therefore, of the budget deficit.[5] Among other things, the debt-neutrality result relies on the fact that consumption depends only on lifetime income and that taxes are not distortionary. In the context of equation (3), distortionary taxes would have an effect on the level of output and investment and would therefore affect the current account. Furthermore, if consumption depends also on disposable income, for example, because some consumers are unable to borrow at the same terms as the government, lower taxes today will induce higher consumption (Jappelli and Pagano, 1994). With respect to the firms, the effective easing of borrowing constraints associated with lower present taxes can similarly induce an increase in investment. Analogous effects will obtain if future tax obligations are not expected to fall entirely on taxpayers in the current period.[6]

---

[5] This result can be understood by considering the effect of public-sector deficits (negative public savings) on private-sector savings. If the private sector fully internalizes the fact that higher deficits today will need to be covered by higher taxation in the future, private savings will rise, to fully offset the negative public savings, without any change in the interest rate (and therefore without any effect on investment). In that case, government bond issues associated with the deficit are not regarded as net wealth and do not influence current private consumption. The invariance of the domestic savings and investment balance implies that the current account is unaffected.

[6] If the future tax obligations arising from the deficit are expected to be met by higher consumption taxes, present consumption would rise (and present savings would fall) as the increase in the relative price of future consumption induces intertemporal substitution of present for future consumption (Frenkel, Razin, and Yuen, 1996). The same argument applies if future tax obligations are to be met with the inflation tax (for example, after the abandonment of an exchange-rate peg). Indeed, if consumers have to hold money balances for consumption purposes, future inflation increases the relative cost of future consumption purchases (Calvo, 1986), thereby encouraging a shift from future to present consumption. Differences between the present and expected future tax burden may be the effect of political factors. Consider, for example, a model in the spirit of Alesina and Tabellini (1990), in which there exists a politically motivated fiscal-deficit bias, caused by the fact that the current government does not share the spending priorities of a possible successor and is therefore willing to commit future tax revenues to debt service, rather than to spending. This will result in future tax rates being higher than current tax rates.

All the effects discussed above imply, among other things, imperfect substitutability between private and public savings and a positive correlation between budget deficits and current-account deficits. The discussion also suggests that the strength of this correlation may depend on the degree of development of the domestic financial markets. In countries with underdeveloped or highly regulated financial markets, for example, we would expect to find stronger links between the fiscal stance and the current-account balance, and therefore between government budget solvency and current-account sustainability. Note also that when current-account deficits are accompanied by large fiscal imbalances, the government faces a "dual transfer" problem—the need to collect resources from the private sector in order to service its external liabilities—which can weaken sustainability (Bevilaqua, 1995).

The amount of private-sector saving offset to a given increase in public-sector saving may also depend on the level of public debt (Sutherland, 1995). If public debt is low, the current generation can view a future debt-stabilization policy (through fiscal surpluses) as remote. Thus, the future tax liabilities are perceived to be small, and fiscal adjustments will affect aggregate demand and savings. If public debt is high, however, the future debt stabilization will appear to be imminent, resulting in debt neutrality. The link between the twin deficits may therefore be stronger the lower is the level of public debt. Another implication of this reasoning is that the higher the public-debt burden, the weaker will be the effects of fiscal stabilization on aggregate demand.

To sum up, large budget deficits may signal problems of fiscal sustainability in the presence of a high substitutability between private and public savings, but they will be only weakly related to current-account developments. If substitutability between private and public savings is low, however, there will be a correlation between fiscal and external sustainability.

Political Instability, Policy Uncertainty, and Credibility

Political economy plays a role in determining the importance of many of the indicators examined so far. In the context of current-account sustainability, political instability can be important for various reasons.

If taxes fall on consumption, intertemporal substitution will push private agents toward higher consumption in the present rather than the future, therefore implying a current-account deficit.

It makes domestic and foreign investors more susceptible to the risk of a sudden policy reversal, reducing the credibility of the current policy stance. A government favoring free capital mobility, for example, may be replaced by one more prone to the imposition of capital controls or to default. This makes the occurrence of capital outflows more likely. Political instability is often driven by distributional conflict, which can cause capital flight as a response to the fear of capital taxation (Alesina and Tabellini, 1989). Numerous empirical studies have documented the association of political instability with high inflation, low investment, and low growth (Cukierman, Edwards, and Tabellini, 1992; Alesina, Özler, Roubini, and Swagel, 1996). Indicators of this kind of political instability are, for example, the historical frequency of changes in government or attempted coups, and measures of industrial strife.

The political situation may affect the sustainability of external liabilities in several ways. A "weak" government may have difficulties undertaking the economic adjustment needed to respond to a shock, because it is unable to gather sufficient political support. A government facing an election may be reluctant to implement adjustment measures for fear of jeopardizing its electoral chances. Indicators of this sort of "policy rigidity" are the degree of support for the government in power, the party composition of the government (coalition as opposed to majority), and the timing of elections.

Although factors such as credibility, political instability, and policy uncertainty influence macroeconomic policy decisions and affect capital flows, it is difficult for our purposes to compress them into simple indicators directly applicable to current-account sustainability.

Market Expectations

A key question in assessing the sustainability of external imbalances is whether it is sufficient to rely on a set of financial-market indicators that signal the likelihood of a major policy shift or crisis situation. Bond prices and interest-rate spreads on international loans and bonds (such as Brady bonds) are useful price measures of the perceptions international investors have of a country's ability to service its external obligations; the behavior of capital flows and foreign-exchange reserves are the most obvious quantity measures of the perceptions of domestic and foreign investors. These financial-market variables should, in principle, reflect all the available information on the external viability of a country, thereby obviating the need to consider additional indicators of sustainability.

Experience suggests, however, that market-based indicators may fail to signal problems in a timely fashion. The ERM and Mexican crises are instructive examples. There are several possible explanations for this failure to signal impending problems. The first is that unexpected shocks may cause the financial markets to revise their rational forecast of a country's ability to defend an exchange-rate peg or to meet external obligations. The second (possibly related) explanation is that expectations of, for example, a collapse of the peg may induce rational herd behavior on the part of investors, so that the belief that the government will have an incentive to abandon the peg if faced with an outflow of capital may become self-fulfilling.[7] In this context, expectations that the peg can hold would also be rational, because the government would have no incentive to abandon it. Clearly, self-fulfilling crises (and, more generally, multiple equilibria) can emerge only under certain configurations of underlying fundamentals. This fact underscores the usefulness of looking at a broader set of indicators for evaluating sustainability.

A third explanation is that, in the presence of imperfect information and noisy signals about a country's liquidity position and creditworthiness, financial-market indicators may fail to perform appropriately as warning signals. Financial markets "get it wrong" at times, and they are prone to irrational herd behavior that tends to exacerbate crises. The absence of "appropriate" price and quantity signals of an impending crisis, however, does not necessarily reflect irrationality in the behavior of foreign lenders. Capital flows and interest-rate premia, for example, may be influenced by (perceived) guarantees of a bailout by creditor countries should a crisis occur. Dooley (1995) follows this reasoning in interpreting commercial-bank lending to developing countries prior to the debt crisis. The discussion suggests the usefulness of considering other measures of sustainability as well, in addition to those offered by the international financial market.

[7] This idea shares many features with models of banks runs (see Diamond and Dybvig, 1983). Obstfeld (1986) presents an early analysis of balance-of-payments crises along these lines. He shows how self-fulfilling crises can occur when government policy decisions reflect well-defined objectives, and he provides an application to the ERM case (Obstfeld, 1994, 1996). Calvo (1988) provides an example of multiple equilibria arising from the need to service the public debt, and Cole and Kehoe (1996) develop a model in which the possibility of a debt crisis depends on the size and maturity structure of external debt. The theory is generally less successful in explaining what triggers the shift between different equilibria.

6 COUNTRY EPISODES

We turn now to a description of a group of countries that have had persistent current-account imbalances. Their experiences fall into three broad categories: (1) episodes in which sustained current-account imbalances have not triggered a sharp policy reversal, (2) episodes in which external or domestic factors have caused a sharp policy reversal but have not led to an external crisis, and (3) episodes in which persistent current-account imbalances have been followed by an external crisis, resulting in debt rescheduling, renegotiations, or a massive bailout. We characterize these various experiences in terms of the macroeconomic policy stance taken, the structural characteristics of the country's economy, and the external shocks affecting the economy. The purpose of the analysis is to identify whether the sustainability indicators (and which of the indicators) help distinguish among the three groups of country episodes and, in particular, among those countries that have experienced external crises and those countries that have not. To interpret the contribution of these indicators to explaining sustainability, it is important to ascertain that differences in the intensity of external shocks are not the predominant reason for the variety of country experiences.

The episodes we consider are those for Australia (1981–1994), Chile (1977–1982), Ireland (1979–1990), Israel (1982–1986), Malaysia I (1979–1986) and II (1991–1995), Mexico I (1977–1982) and II (1991–1995), and South Korea (1978–1988). The experiences of these countries can be broadly characterized as follows. Australia and Malaysia (1991–1995) showed persistent current-account deficits but no drastic policy changes. Ireland, Israel, Malaysia (1984–1985), and South Korea all showed a policy reversal (triggered by external or domestic imbalances) that prevented potential external crises. Chile and Mexico I and II suffered external crises. The brief country studies below are accompanied by figures describing the evolution in each country of investment, national saving, the current account, and the real exchange rate.

Australia: 1981–1994

Australia (Figure 2) has run current-account deficits for the past forty years almost without interruption (the exception being 1973). Indeed, the impact of persistent current-account imbalances has long been at

31

the center of the economic-policy debate in Australia (Pitchford, 1989; Corden, 1991). The average size of Australia's deficits has been close to 5 percent of GDP since the early 1980s, considerably higher than in previous decades. At the end of the 1970s, Australia's net external position was characterized by low external debt (6 percent of GDP, 25 percent of net external liabilities), because the capital inflows that financed the current-account imbalances took mainly the form of equity. In 1982–83, Australia experienced a recession but rapidly recovered and showed output growth averaging 4.5 percent for the rest of the decade. At the end of 1983, the exchange rate, which had followed a crawling peg since 1976, was floated. Following a negative terms-of-trade shock in 1985–86, current-account imbalances grew worse and the deficit increased to nearly 6 percent of GDP. The current-account deficit narrowed somewhat during the next two years as the terms of trade improved, but it widened again significantly in 1989. This increase in imbalances occurred despite a tightening of fiscal policy that started in 1984 and led to a surplus by 1989. The rise in public savings was offset by an increase in private spending, in particular on investment. The persistent current-account imbalances and the shift toward debt financing resulted in an increase in the ratio of external debt to GDP to over 30 percent by the end of 1989, with debt service absorbing 20 percent of total export receipts.

The 1990s started with a recession, triggered by a fall in business investment, a depreciation in the real exchange rate, and a decline in prices of commercial property, all of which resulted in a sharp increase in unemployment. Output subsequently recovered, driven mainly by increases in private consumption and net exports as the real exchange rate continued to depreciate. In 1994, growth accelerated to about 5 percent, driven by buoyant domestic demand. The investment share of GDP, however, failed to regain the levels reached in the 1980s. The fiscal balance, which had registered a surplus until 1990, returned to a deficit, which was close to 6 percent in 1993; current-account imbalances again widened and reached 5 percent in 1995.

What are the main characteristics of Australia's external position? During the 1980s, following the worldwide deregulation of financial markets and the removal of capital controls, capital flows into Australia took mainly the form of debt. During the last five years, current-account imbalances have, instead, been financed primarily by net equity flows, and debt accumulation has been quite modest. Indeed, Australia stands out among the industrial countries for the large proportion of its external liabilities that take the form of equity. The ratio

FIGURE 2

AUSTRALIA

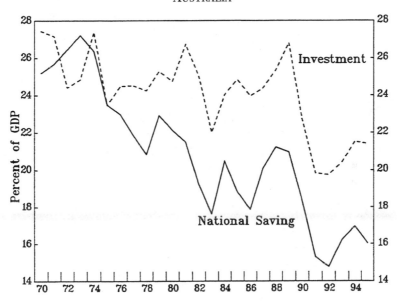

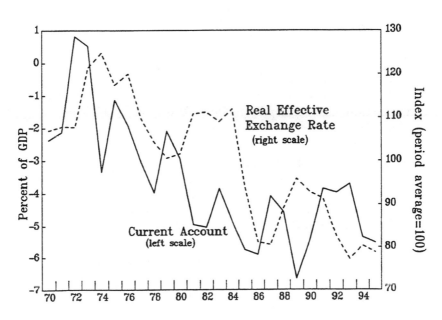

SOURCE: International Monetary Fund.

of external debt to GDP stood at 36 percent at the end of 1994, with two-thirds of the debt reflecting private obligations; in 1993, interest payments on external debt were about 2 percent of GDP. Because over 40 percent of this debt is denominated in Australian dollars, the external position of the economy is less vulnerable to fluctuations in the exchange rate.

A salient feature of the Australian economy is the floating-exchange-rate regime, which makes the economy less vulnerable to a balance-of-payments crisis. The real effective exchange rate is currently more depreciated than its historical average. The degree of openness has increased over time, with the export ratio rising from 15 percent in the early 1980s to about 20 percent in 1994. The composition of exports has been changing, with the importance of wool and other agricultural products declining and exports of minerals and manufactures increasing. The economy nevertheless remains vulnerable to swings in the terms of trade. The investment ratio, which averaged 24 percent over the 1980s, declined to an average of 20 percent for the period from 1990 to 1994; the GDP share of national savings also declined, to an average of 16.5 percent during the latter period. The growth rate of the Australian economy has nevertheless exceeded the OECD average over the past ten years. These factors point to a sustainable current-account position, despite the decline in savings and investment.

Chile: 1977–1982

The first half of the 1970s was a turbulent period for Chile both politically and economically (Figure 3). The coup in 1973 ousted Allende's socialist government and installed a military regime that had radically different economic policies. After a period during which the government's role in the economy had steadily increased, the new regime strived to balance the budget and to advance privatization and financial and trade liberalization. As a result of this tightening of domestic policy, as well as of external shocks such as the fall in the price of copper and increase in the price of oil, the economy endured a severe recession in 1974–75.

By 1978, yearly inflation in Chile was reduced from over 400 percent in 1973 to 30 percent, the public sector was in surplus (1.5 percent of GDP), and the economy was growing at 8 percent. The rise in investment and the low level of private savings, however, implied a large current-account deficit (5 percent of GDP). The unemployment rate, moreover, stood above 14 percent. Following the adoption of a schedule of preannounced devaluations of the nominal exchange rate (the *tablita*)

34

FIGURE 3

CHILE

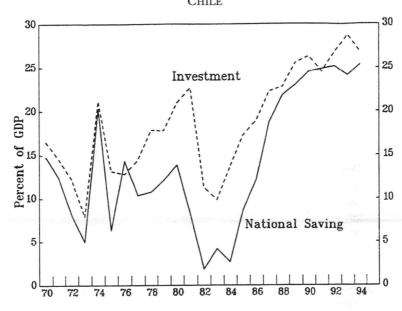

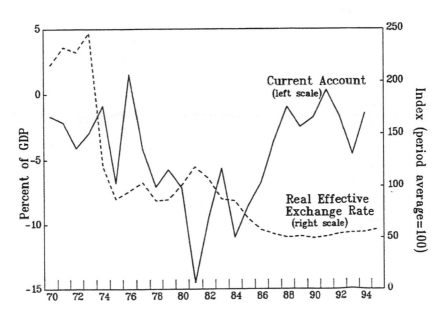

SOURCE: International Monetary Fund.

for a year and a half, the government chose to use the exchange rate as a full-fledged nominal anchor in the disinflation process. In June 1979, it fixed the rate against the dollar. Although the strong recovery continued over the following years, inflation declined rather slowly, with full backward-looking indexation slowing its descent (Edwards and Cox-Edwards, 1987). The inflationary process was sustained by monetary growth caused by large capital inflows reflecting private-sector external borrowing used to finance investment in the wake of financial liberalization.[1] The real exchange rate appreciated rapidly by consequence, and the current-account balance deteriorated, with the ratio of the deficit to GDP reaching double digits in 1981.

By late 1981, wholesale prices in Chile were falling, but the magnitude of the cumulative real appreciation caused expectations of a devaluation and, therefore, of a widening of interest-rate spreads between peso- and dollar-denominated assets. Output began to decline and unemployment increased. In 1982, a sequence of external events—a sharp decline in the terms of trade, the large increase in world interest rates, and a drying up of external sources of financing following the Mexican debt crisis—forced the government to abandon its exchange-rate peg. In June 1982, the exchange rate was devalued by 18 percent, and wage indexation was abandoned. This was not, however, sufficient. As in Mexico in 1994, speculation against the peso increased, and reserves declined rapidly. Toward the end of 1982, in the wake of an impending financial crisis, the government imposed capital controls and import surcharges. By June of 1983, the peso had been devalued in nominal terms by close to 100 percent with respect to the previous year's level.

The crisis caused widespread bankruptcies in the private sector, and the government was forced to liquidate banks and to bail out several other financial and nonfinancial institutions. In particular, the central bank intervened in support of the banking system, giving rise to a large quasi-fiscal deficit. Despite the absence of government guarantees on private foreign borrowing, the government assumed responsibility for a large portion of the private sector's foreign liabilities. The crisis was severe: output fell by 14 percent in 1983 alone, and unemployment rose

---

[1] As Edwards and Cox-Edwards (1987), among others, point out, private foreign borrowing did not carry government guarantees. A significant portion of foreign borrowing was carried out by the so-called *grupos*—large conglomerates that included industrial firms as well as banks. These conglomerates had been major buyers of privatized firms, and the banks extended most of their lending to firms within the same conglomerate, thereby circumventing lax regulations.

to close to 20 percent (Corbo and Fischer, 1994). Inflation rebounded to 27 percent, and the management of the crisis caused an initial reversal with respect to exchange-rate policy, wage indexation, current- and capital-account openness, and privatization. Starting in 1984, however, the government resumed its program of trade liberalization, privatization, and deregulation, and the adjustment of the Chilean economy, although painful, was relatively rapid. Growth resumed in 1984 and averaged over 6 percent over the next ten years.

It should be noted that not all the indicators discussed above pointed to the likelihood of a crisis. The economy was experiencing rapid economic growth; the fiscal balance was in surplus throughout the period (indeed, the government had been reducing its external liabilities), investment was growing rapidly (albeit from a low base), and so were exports (until 1981). Which factors, then, explain the Chilean crisis in 1982? Those most commonly mentioned are (1) *the size of external debt*—external indebtedness was close to 50 percent of GDP in 1981, with interest payments reaching 5.5 percent of GDP; (2) *an overvalued real exchange rate*—the effects of lagged wage indexation and the increased demand for nontradables fueled by foreign borrowing prevented inflation from converging rapidly to world levels. Investment was stimulated by a reduction in the price of imported capital goods, as well as by the possibility, given the pegged exchange rate, of obtaining financing on world markets at the world rate of interest; (3) *the low level of savings*—national savings averaged only 10 percent of GDP from 1978 to 1981. The decline, particularly significant in 1981, may have reflected the effects of intertemporal substitution; (4) *weakness in the financial system and overborrowing*—overborrowing by the private sector was fueled by the availability of foreign credit (following the recycling of oil exporters' surpluses) and was facilitated by weak supervision of the banking sector, which encouraged risk-taking behavior (Diaz-Alejandro, 1985; Velasco, 1991). De la Cuadra and Valdes-Prieto (1992) stress the negative role played in this regard by the government's extension to the private sector of guarantees against exchange-rate and interest-rate risk; and (5) *severe external shocks*—the large increase in world interest rates, the drying up of foreign financing, and the decline in the terms of trade (compounded by a narrow commodity export base dominated by copper) all contributed to precipitating the external crisis.

Ireland: 1979–1990

Ireland (Figure 4) is an interesting case of a country that has persistently large current-account imbalances and a consequently large external debt, but that has achieved a remarkable reversal in its external accounts. As in the Israeli case, this reversal was the result of a drastic fiscal-stabilization plan that reversed the rising trend in the ratio of public debt to GDP (see Dornbusch, 1989, Giavazzi and Pagano, 1990, and Walsh, 1996, for more detailed accounts).

Ireland's external imbalances grew dramatically worse following the second oil shock in 1979–80. Although exports had increased throughout the 1970s, imports had risen more rapidly. By 1979, the current-account deficit was about 13 percent of GDP, and it remained above 10 percent for the next three years. This deterioration reflected a continuing decline in the ratio of public savings to GDP, as well as a fall in private savings that more than offset a decline in the share of investment to GDP. As a result, the government's external public debt doubled as a fraction of GDP between 1979 and 1982, to 40 percent; inflation accelerated to over 20 percent in 1981; and the fiscal deficit reached 12 percent. To face these growing macroeconomic imbalances, the government implemented a fiscal-adjustment plan in 1982 that was accompanied by a sharp disinflation strategy centered on pegging the Irish punt within the European Monetary System. By 1984, the full-employment primary deficit had been substantially reduced, thanks primarily to tax increases (Giavazzi and Pagano, 1990), and inflation had fallen below 10 percent. A substantial fall in private consumption and investment and an export boom, driven by large increases in manufacturing exports, resulted in a remarkable shift in the trade balance, from a deficit of over 12 percent of GDP in 1981 to a surplus of 1 percent in 1984.[2]

The high-interest burden and the appreciation of the U.S. dollar during these years implied an increase in the ratio of public external debt to GDP to almost 50 percent by 1984. Despite Ireland's fiscal-adjustment effort, the domestic public debt also kept rising, and the ratio of total debt to GDP reached 125 percent in 1987. In that year, the government implemented another plan for fiscal stabilization. This plan relied more heavily on expenditure cuts than the previous plan had and, in order to stimulate exports, devalued the exchange rate before the fiscal contraction. The stabilization reduced fiscal imbalances by 9 percentage points of GDP (8 of which consisted of primary balance)

---

[2] Manufacturing exports in Ireland are mainly produced by foreign firms. Since its entry into the European Community in 1973, Ireland has been the recipient of large flows in foreign direct investment.

FIGURE 4
IRELAND

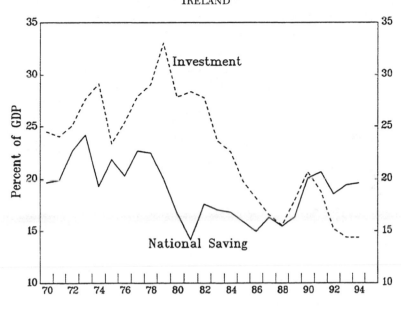

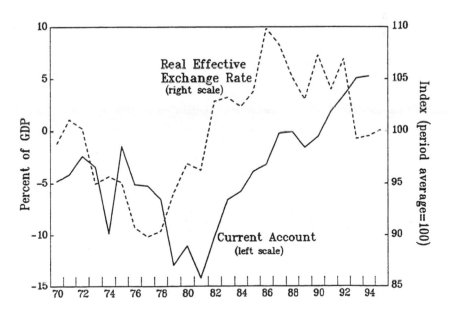

SOURCE: International Monetary Fund.

between 1986 and 1989, reversing the increasing trend of the ratio of public debt to GDP.[3] The economy, spurred by very favorable external developments, grew at an average rate of over 4 percent between 1988 and 1994, and gross public debt declined to about 90 percent by 1994.

The stabilization was accompanied by another drastic improvement in the current-account balance, thanks to an increase in the trade surplus to over 10 percent of GDP. Once again, exports of manufactures expanded rapidly; in 1991, they accounted for over 40 percent of GDP. As a result, Ireland ran a current-account surplus for the first time in twenty years.

Some specific features of the Irish experience should be noted. Foreign direct investment has clearly played a pivotal role in Ireland. It has decisively contributed to the increase in export orientation and to the change in the composition of exports away from agricultural toward manufactured goods. By 1990, foreign firms accounted for about one-half of Ireland's manufacturing gross output and over 75 percent of its manufacturing exports (OECD, 1993). As a consequence, the current-account balance shows a sizable deficit in net factor income, caused by interest on foreign borrowing and, especially, by profit repatriation, and there is a large difference between gross domestic product and gross national product (GNP)—over 11 percent in 1993. The current-account deficit is in part offset by large net current transfers, in particular from the European Union, which amounted to over 6 percent of GNP in 1993.

In summary, Ireland's large external imbalances in the early and mid-1980s were clearly associated with an unsustainable fiscal-policy stance. The drastic contraction in fiscal policy was accompanied by strong export-led growth that helped reverse the pattern of large persistent external deficits.[4] The increase in exports was itself stimulated by the 1987 devaluation, which made the real exchange rate competitive. Favorable external conditions (the boom in the United Kingdom and the United States, the fall in commodity prices and world interest rates) also played an important role. The large increase in unemployment, only partly reabsorbed, and the large decline in the investment share (from over 30 percent in the late 1970s to 15 percent in 1993) are the lingering negative aspects of a successful adjustment strategy.

[3] The ratio of public external debt to GDP also declined. Because there was an increase during this period in foreigners' holdings of punt-denominated securities, the decline in foreign-currency debt overstates the actual decline in public external debt.

[4] There is a debate regarding the degree to which transfer pricing, encouraged by favorable tax treatment of capital, increases recorded exports. Even after "correcting" Ireland's exports for profit repatriation, however, the increase in exports is remarkable.

Israel: 1982–1986

Except for the years from 1986 to 1989, Isreal has run persistent current-account deficits, despite large unilateral transfers from abroad (Figure 5). Economic growth, sustained by periodic waves of immigration and by high investment rates, averaged 10 percent until the early 1970s, a level that was resumed in the early 1990s. During the 1970s and 1980s, however, growth was much more modest, and the sustainability of external imbalances came into question, particularly with regard to two episodes. The first of these, in 1973–1974, was characterized by the increase in oil prices and by the Yom Kippur war; the second began in 1979 but lasted until the mid-1980s. We focus here on the second episode.

From 1979 to mid–1985, the Israeli economy experienced low growth, high inflation, large fiscal imbalances (about 15 percent of GDP) and large current-account deficits. As a result, domestic and foreign public debt accumulated rapidly. The dramatic acceleration of inflation that year, to over 400 percent per annum, underscored the need for drastic stabilization measures. In June of 1985, an inflation-stabilization plan was implemented. The program fixed the exchange rate (following a big devaluation), tightened monetary policy, and imposed a massive fiscal adjustment (including expenditure cuts, tax increases, and increased transfers from abroad) that eliminated the budget deficit (Bruno, 1993; Bufman and Leiderman, 1995). Inflation declined abruptly to between 15 and 20 percent. An additional benefit of the plan was a remarkable reversal in external accounts. The current account, which had shown an average deficit of over 7 percent of GDP over the previous three years, showed a surplus of almost 5 percent of GDP in 1985. The adjustment defused the risk of excessive external indebtedness, reducing the ratio of foreign public debt to GDP from 84 percent of GDP in 1984 to about 30 percent by 1990 (the net external debt to GDP dropped from 48 percent in 1984 to 28 percent in 1991).

What accounted for the shift in the current-account balance? Investment declined sharply, whereas national savings and international transfers increased. The drop in private savings, reflecting a consumption boom following the stabilization plan, was more than offset by the increase in public savings. Clearly, the increase in international transfers facilitated the adjustment of the Israeli economy to a low-inflation environment by obviating the need for even more drastic fiscal-adjustment measures. The competitiveness of the export sector was at a historical peak, enhanced by the up-front depreciation in the exchange rate, the de-indexation of wages, and the fiscal consolidation (Figure 5).

FIGURE 5
ISRAEL

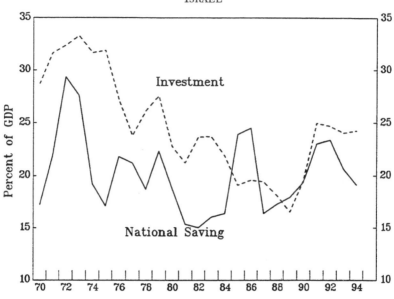

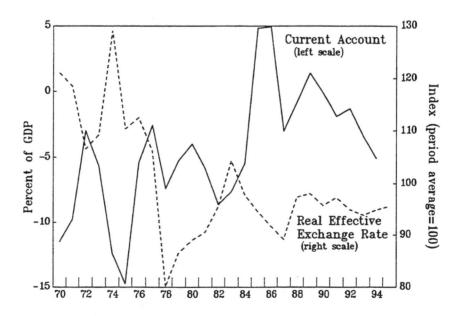

SOURCE: International Monetary Fund.

More generally, the economy showed a high degree of openness and was favored by free-trade agreements with the European Community and the United States. In the following years, international transfers fell as a proportion of GDP, investment rates remained low, and national savings remained stable, although at a higher level than during the inflationary period.

In contrast to other countries in our sample, the fiscal and current-account adjustment process in Israel was not triggered by unfavorable external shocks. Indeed, the adjustment was actually facilitated by external developments (the increase in transfers and the decline in oil prices in 1986); it could be seen as an example of "expansionary fiscal consolidation" (Razin and Sadka, 1996).

Malaysia I: 1979–1986

At the end of the 1970s, Malaysia's macroeconomic situation was stable (Demery and Demery, 1992). The economy had grown at an average rate of over 6 percent during the 1970s. Inflation was low, exports were increasing rapidly, external debt was low, and current-account surpluses were substantial (Figure 6). The country had begun to diversify its production and exports away from primary commodities toward manufactured goods and textiles, although primary commodities still accounted for over 70 percent of Malaysia's total exports in 1980.

The oil shock of 1979–80 implied a sharp improvement in the terms of trade. At about the same time, there was a shift in the government's macroeconomic policy stance. The government began to promote a drive toward heavy industry, similar to that pursued by South Korea a few years earlier. The drive, which was pursued through large invest-ment projects undertaken both directly and through state-owned enterprises, led to a rapid increase in the share of public investment in GDP and a widening of the federal budget deficit from 6.6 percent of GDP in 1980 to over 17 percent in 1982. About 40 percent of the deficit was financed through external borrowing. The deterioration in the fiscal accounts was mirrored by external developments. The deficit on the current account reached 13 percent of GDP in 1982, resulting in a sharp increase in external debt, to 47 percent of GDP. The deficit also reflected unfavorable external conditions. The slowdown in the world economy, the increase in world real interest rates, a progressive deterioration in the terms of trade, and an appreciation of the real exchange rate all had an effect.

Worries about the rapid rise in domestic and external imbalances prompted the Malaysian government to undertake a program of fiscal consolidation characterized by a curtailment of public-sector investment. Development expenditure was reduced by 30 percent in nominal terms during 1983–84; the federal deficit was reduced to 7 percent of GDP; and the current-account deficit was reduced to 6 percent of GDP by 1984. The macroeconomic effects of fiscal adjustment were cushioned in part by a temporary reversal in the deterioration of the terms of trade in 1984, a recovery in world demand, and a sustained expansion of Malaysia's manufacturing and construction sectors; as a result, the Malaysian economy continued to grow at a rapid pace.

Economic activity experienced a sharp decline in 1985 and 1986, however, reflecting a marked deterioration of external conditions (a substantial worsening in the terms of trade and weak external demand), further fiscal tightening, and an abrupt slowdown in construction activity. Public investment was further reduced. At the same time, monetary policy was loosened, interest rates were allowed to decline, and the exchange rate depreciated substantially. The slowdown was accompanied by severe problems in the financial system, triggered by the collapse in the real-estate market. The combined effect of the large depreciation in the real exchange rate and the fiscal contraction led to a reduction in absorption and to a shifting of expenditures. Imports declined significantly, and exports increased. Although weakness in economic activity limited the size of the deficit adjustment, a sharp fall in private consumption and private investment implied a virtual balancing of the current account in 1986. Beginning in 1987, economic activity recovered, and for the rest of the decade, the current-account balance recorded large surpluses, reflecting a large increase in the savings rate (Figure 7). This increase allowed Malaysia to reduce its external debt substantially.

What are the salient features of the Malaysian experience? The rapid buildup in domestic and external debt during the early 1980s required a drastic policy shift to ensure fiscal and external sustainability. This shift involved not only fiscal consolidation, but also structural measures to encourage private-sector investment. The prolonged period of fiscal adjustment took its toll on economic activity in 1985–86, when domestic and external conditions deteriorated. The downturn was rapidly reversed, however, as the sharp depreciation in the real exchange rate and the more favorable environment for private-sector investment allowed growth to resume. The remarkable reversal in the current-account balance between 1983 and 1987 (from a deficit of 12 percent of GDP to a surplus of 8 percent) reflected higher savings, but also a large

44

FIGURE 6

MALAYSIA

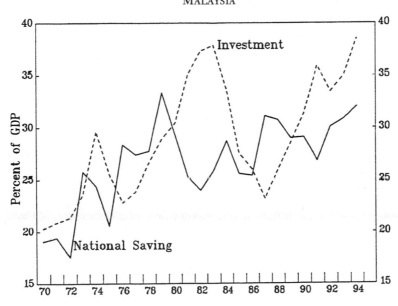

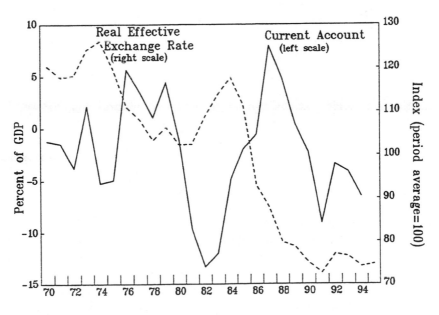

SOURCE: International Monetary Fund.

decline in the share of investment, from almost 38 percent of GDP in 1983 to 23 percent in 1987 (Fry, 1993).

Malaysia II: 1991–1995

The macroeconomic environment was different in the early 1990s, when the second episode of large current-account deficits occurred in Malaysia. The 1990s have been characterized by high growth driven by booming private investment and exports (helped by rapid growth among East Asian trading partners) and by large surpluses in the capital account. The share of investment in GDP reached 38 percent in 1994, with private investment accounting for two-thirds of the total. A rising fraction of this investment reflected inflows in the form of foreign direct investment, in particular from Japan and other, newly industrialized, Asian countries. Exports grew rapidly (to 82 percent of GDP by 1994), especially exports of manufactured goods, which accounted for close to 80 percent of total exports. The private investment boom encouraged rapid growth in imports, particularly of intermediate and capital goods, and this caused a narrowing of the trade surplus. The economic-policy stance also differed from that of the early 1980s. Fiscal policy was much more restrained. The ratio of public debt to GDP steadily declined, and monetary policy was directed toward controlling monetary aggregates in the face of substantial capital inflows while resisting a sharp appreciation of the exchange rate.

Large capital inflows began in 1990 and increased significantly in the following years. In 1993 alone, the capital-account surplus was over 20 percent of GDP. Long-term flows remained relatively stable from 1992 to 1994, but the importance of short-term capital inflows (mainly changes in the net-foreign-asset position of financial institutions, as well as portfolio investment) increased significantly in 1992 and 1993. The monetary authorities reacted by trying to sterilize the inflows. As a result, between 1991 and 1993, the total accumulation of foreign-exchange reserves was $17 billion, or 16 percent of GDP per year.[5] The size of the capital inflows and, in particular, the large short-term component, prompted the authorities to adopt a series of measures in early 1994 directed at discouraging short-term flows. As a result, there was a large outflow of short-term capital in 1994; long-term flows—including foreign direct investment—were unaffected. The real effective exchange rate depreciated slightly, after having appreciated from 1991 to 1993. In 1995, a continuation of rapid growth and booming investment widened current-account imbalances further, to an estimated level of 8.3 percent of GDP.

[5] Here and throughout, billion equals a thousand million.

Despite its large and protracted current-account deficits, Malaysia has avoided a rapid accumulation of external debt. Its ratio of external debt to GDP has remained broadly stable, thanks to large non-debt-creating inflows, and its debt burden, measured by interest payments as a ratio of GDP, has steadily declined. In comparison to other countries in our sample, Malaysia has high levels of investment and savings, a high ratio of exports to GDP, and a stable real exchange rate, factors that would point to a sustainable external position. In comparison to Malaysia's own earlier episode, fiscal imbalances are moderate, private investment more prominent, the real exchange rate more competitive, and the economy less vulnerable to shifts in commodity prices.

Mexico I: 1977-1982

After a long period of sustained economic growth, low, stable inflation, and an exchange rate fixed against the U.S. dollar, the Mexican economy went through a period of increased macroeconomic instability at the beginning of the 1970s (Figure 8). Public expenditure increased substantially, and inflation accelerated, causing the real exchange rate to appreciate. As a result, external debt accumulated rapidly. In 1976, the exchange-rate peg collapsed under mounting balance-of-payments pressures, and the peso was devalued by almost 100 percent. The government imposed import controls and, later in the year, reached agreement on a stabilization package with the IMF.

In 1977, when it became known that the Mexican oil reserves were nearly two and a half times the amount estimated in 1975 (16 billion barrels as opposed to 6.4 billion barrels), the government changed its policy stance. As foreign banks competed to lend to Mexico on very attractive terms, the constraints on foreign borrowing were lifted. Public expenditure once again increased, from 29 percent of GDP in 1977 to 41 percent in 1981, with state-owned enterprises taking an important role in public investment. From 1978 to 1981, public and private investment rose rapidly, and growth climbed above 8 percent. Although private savings increased, public-sector savings declined significantly. This, together with the investment boom, was reflected in large current-account deficits (over 6 percent of GDP in 1981). As a result, external debt almost doubled in dollar terms between 1979 and 1981.

Although domestic inflation climbed rapidly past 20 percent, the nominal exchange rate was devalued more slowly, a combination that resulted in a large real appreciation. During 1981, it became clear that the earlier assumptions regarding the rate of increase of oil-export revenues were unrealistic. This fueled speculation that the peso would

47

FIGURE 7

MEXICO

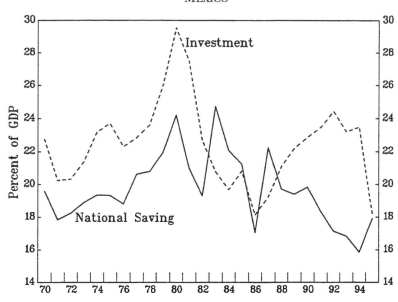

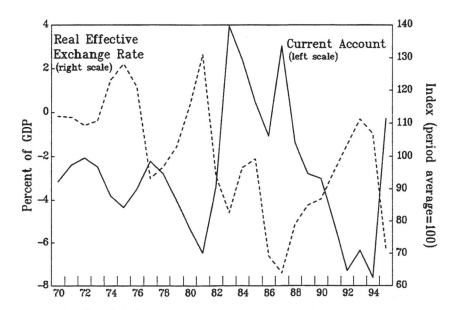

SOURCE: International Monetary Fund.

be devalued, causing massive capital flight. To stem the drain of foreign-exchange reserves, the government increased its external borrowing by over $20 billion. The terms of the debt began to worsen, however, with a shortening of debt maturities and an increase in the spreads over the London interbank offer rate (LIBOR), at a time when the LIBOR itself was increasing.

The crisis worsened in 1982, as a result of external shocks (the increase in world real interest rates and the world recession) and increasing fiscal imbalances. A 40 percent devaluation of the peso in February stemmed capital flight only briefly, and the government had to borrow an additional $5.7 billion in medium-term, syndicated loans. In August, a dual exchange-rate system was established. Shortly thereafter, dollar deposits at Mexican commercial banks were converted into pesos at an unfavorable exchange rate, and on September 1, the banking system was nationalized. During the last four months of the year, there was a *de facto* moratorium on foreign-debt service, until an agreement to reschedule $23 billion of debt amortization was reached with foreign commercial banks in December.

In 1983, the new De la Madrid administration implemented a drastic adjustment plan that included a fiscal contraction, a lifting of previously adopted trade restrictions, and a reduction in real wages. The change in the current account was immediate. It registered a surplus, although this came at a heavy price. Output contracted by over 5 percent in 1983, and public and private investment fell dramatically.

What were the main aspects of the Mexican crisis in 1982, aside from external shocks and the high level of external indebtedness? The literature mentions four factors:[6] (1) *appreciation in the real exchange rate*—between 1977 and 1981, Mexico's exchange rate appreciated against the dollar by over 30 percent in real terms (Buffie, 1989). This appreciation stimulated a boom in imports, which increased much faster than oil exports. The perception that the exchange rate was unsustainable led to substantial capital flight during the years preceding the crisis, as well during the following years; (2) *large fiscal imbalances*—most of the debt accumulation in Mexico reflected external borrowing by the public sector. The increase in public expenditure

[6] Some observers attribute the debt crisis primarily to external factors and emphasize that several distinguished commentators (and the commercial banks themselves) argued at the time that there was no reason to worry, because the current-account deficits were financing higher public and private investment (Diaz-Alejandro, 1984). Indeed, Mexico's macroeconomic performance between 1978 and 1981 was very good, showing high growth and rapid increases in public and private investment.

during the late 1970s and early 1980s was extremely large, and it came on top of a previous large increase in the early 1970s. Public expenditure financed not only increased public investment, moreover, but also growing public consumption. Despite the large increase in revenue coming from oil, total revenues failed to keep up with expenditures, creating a large deficit gap. The government's external position was made worse by the fact that external borrowing by the public sector financed not only fiscal imbalances, but also private-capital flight, as foreign-exchange reserves became rapidly depleted; (3) *misperceptions regarding oil wealth*—policy design in Mexico was based on an overoptimistic assessment of future oil prices. When the expected price increases failed to materialize, the government did not introduce alternative measures to limit fiscal imbalances; (4) *weakness of the financial system*—the Mexican financial system was highly repressed and had high reserve requirements, meant mainly to facilitate the financing of public-sector deficits. The sharp deterioration in macroeconomic conditions in 1982 worsened the balance sheets of banks and firms, which were further affected in their dollar exposure by the exchange-rate depreciation.

Mexico II: 1991–1994

The Mexican economy experienced large structural changes during the late 1980s and early 1990s. A change in monetary and fiscal policy was followed by the restructuring of the external debt, the privatization of public enterprises and nationalized banks, and by the liberalization of trade. The results were remarkable. Economic growth averaged 3.5 percent from 1989 to 1992, inflation fell from 160 percent in 1987 to single digits in 1993, and the overall balance of the public sector improved by 13 percent of GDP. In addition, foreign debt declined relative to GDP—from 50 percent in 1988 to 22 percent in 1992—thanks to the agreement on debt restructuring, the appreciation of the real exchange rate, and economic growth. The exchange rate, which was used as a nominal anchor in the disinflation process, appreciated by over 60 percent between 1987 and 1992.

In the aftermath of the debt-restructuring agreement, Mexico regained access to international capital markets. Net capital inflows increased dramatically from 1990 to 1993, totaling over $90 billion (an average of 6 percent of GDP per year), or roughly one-fifth of all net inflows to developing countries. Net foreign direct investment during this period was about $17 billion, and inflows from portfolio investment were more than $60 billion (IMF, 1995a).

Gross domestic investment recovered to 23 percent of GDP in 1992. Despite a large increase in government savings, however, national savings fell sharply, and the current-account deficit reached almost 7 percent of GDP in 1992 (Figure 8). The capital-account surplus, however, was more than sufficient to finance the deficit and to allow for the rapid accumulation of reserves. After a slowdown in 1993, when output growth fell below 1 percent, the economy recovered in 1994; output grew at 3.5 percent, a level sustained by a rapid growth in exports (over 14 percent in dollar terms). Imports continued to grow even more rapidly, however, and the current-account deficit widened to 8 percent of GDP.

Financial-market developments turned unfavorable in 1994. A series of domestic and external shocks (the peasant revolt in Chiapas in January, the assassination of presidential candidate Colosio in March, and the increase in U.S. interest rates in early 1994), as well as a change in the policy stance in the run-up to the August 1994 presidential election caused a loss of confidence on the part of international financial markets and a reversal in capital flows. The exchange rate was allowed to depreciate in real terms within its band, and the Banco de Mexico sterilized the impact of the loss of reserves on money supply. The level of reserves remained fairly stable until October, reflecting a moderate resumption of capital inflows during the third quarter. Between March and November, however, the authorities reacted to an increase in the interest differential between short-term public debt denominated in pesos (cetes) and dollars (tesobonos) by increasing the share of dollar-denominated tesobonos in total government debt outstanding from 6 percent at the end of February to 50 percent at the end of November.

The crisis unfolded quickly. At the end of November, tensions resurfaced on foreign-exchange markets, and the Banco de Mexico again lost reserves. In an attempt to stem foreign-exchange pressures, the fluctuation band for the peso was widened by 15 percent on December 19. The adjustment, however, was insufficient. The peso reached the new edge of the band within two days, and reserves were drained trying to maintain the exchange rate at the band's edge. On December 22, the government announced that the peso would be allowed to float against the U.S. dollar. The Mexican currency plummeted as doubts surfaced about the ability of Mexico to service its short-term liabilities. Despite an international rescue package put together at the end of January, 1995 was a very difficult year for the Mexican economy; bankruptcies were widespread, as was financial distress, and economic activity sharply declined.

51

There are several, to some degree complementary, explanations of the crisis (IMF, 1995b, gives an early assessment). Dornbusch, Goldfajn, and Valdes (1995) argue that the use of the peso as a nominal anchor in the disinflation process had led, in the presence of sticky prices, to overvaluation and to large current-account deficits that were ultimately unsustainable. An exchange-rate correction was, therefore, overdue, as Dornbusch and Werner (1994) had suggested before the crisis. The domestic political shocks and the external shocks simply exposed the underlying vulnerability of the Mexican economy.[7]

An alternative, but possibly complementary, view stresses policy inconsistencies that emerged in 1994—in particular the monetary-policy stance and the management of the public debt—as well as a shift in investors' sentiment. Once capital inflows stopped in the second quarter of 1994, following the increase in U.S. interest rates and political disorder in Mexico, the current-account deficit led to a loss in reserves. The sterilization of reserve losses by the Banco de Mexico, however, prevented interest rates from affecting the direction of capital flows and from influencing the current-account balance through a dampening of economic activity.[8] The large conversion of short-term domestic-currency debt, moreover, into short-term dollar-denominated public debt implied an increasing stock of short-term liabilities denominated in foreign exchange that could be "redeemed" at the central bank in exchange for reserves (Sachs, Tornell, and Velasco, 1996; Calvo and Mendoza, 1996a).

How does the Mexican experience relate to the sustainability indicators discussed in Chapter 5? The ratios of foreign debt to GDP and to exports (34.7 percent and 184 percent, respectively) were not excessively high by historical terms or by comparison with other heavily indebted middle-income developing countries. Fiscal policy, a clear culprit of the previous two Mexican crises, had been restrained for the previous four years. Exports, although still low as a fraction of GDP,

---

[7] Dornbusch, Goldfajn, and Valdes (1995) recognize that the current-account deficit and the appreciation of the real exchange rate were, to some degree, the logical consequence of the productivity increases facilitated by the implementation of large market-oriented reforms, the access to the North American Free Trade Agreement, and the reductions in inflation and the size of the public sector. In this context, the increase in permanent income led private agents to raise their levels of consumption, whereas the increase in output surfaced more slowly, because of lags associated with investment and the intersectoral reallocation of resources induced by trade liberalization and changes in relative prices. The question is to what degree the real appreciation reflected a misalignment.

[8] The reluctance of the monetary authorities to raise domestic interest rates was allegedly driven by the fragile situation of the banking system. A drastic increase in interest rates, however, was later forced on the authorities by the currency crisis.

were still growing strongly in 1994.[9] The banking system was, however, weak, and had a large proportion of bad loans and a mismatch between the maturity structure of assets and liabilities. In addition, the national savings rate had declined to very low levels, and the real exchange rate was overvalued, at least to some degree (although there is disagreement on what would have been the appropriate way to "unwind" the overvaluation). Finally, the impending election made it even more difficult to adjust policy to address the series of domestic and external shocks that hit the economy during 1994.

South Korea: 1978–1988

During the 1960s and 1970s, South Korea experienced rapid growth rates driven by investment and exports.[10] It also experienced persistent current-account deficits. Foreign indebtedness, after rising sharply during the time of the first oil crisis, remained stable as a fraction of GDP, at about 32 percent in the latter part of the 1970s, thanks to the high growth rate and low or negative real interest rates. The second oil shock, however, hit the South Korean economy at a particularly delicate juncture. The shock was preceded by a period of real-exchange-rate appreciation, caused by high domestic inflation coupled with a fixed rate against the U.S. dollar, and it coincided with a bad harvest and a period of political instability following the assassination of President Park in October 1979. As a result, the economy suffered a large recession in 1980. The current-account deficit rose to over 8 percent of GDP as household savings declined sharply, and the ratio of foreign debt to GDP increased to 44 percent.

The government's response to the recession was swift and comprehensive. It devalued the exchange rate, tightened macroeconomic policy, and implemented structural reforms such as trade and financial liberalization. Economic growth resumed in 1981, and the fiscal stance was relaxed. During the adjustment period, South Korea continued to borrow on international markets and to finance large current-account deficits. In 1982, the ratio of foreign debt to GDP reached 52 percent.

---

[9] The ratio of exports to GDP in Mexico differs depending on whether it is calculated using national-income accounts or balance-of-payments statistics (as reported in the IMF's *International Financial Statistics*). Using national-income accounts, the ratio of exports of goods and services to GDP was 12.4 percent in 1993. Using balance-of-payments statistics, it was 17 percent. The number reported in Table 2 corresponds to the national income accounts' calculation.

[10] For analyses of the South Korean experience, see Aghevli and Márquez-Ruarte (1985), Collins and Park (1989), SaKong (1993), Soon (1993), and Haggard et al. (1994).

FIGURE 8
SOUTH KOREA

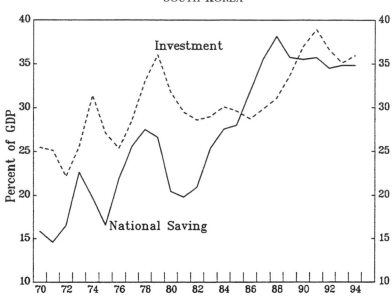

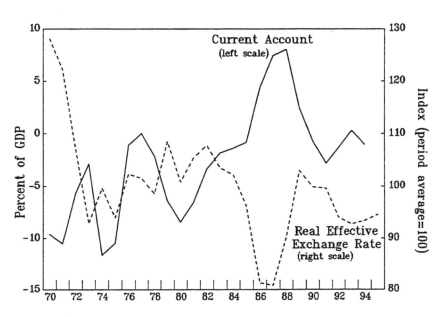

SOURCE: International Monetary Fund.

With strong growth under way and external demand increasing, South Korea turned to reducing the ratio of foreign debt to GDP. It tightened monetary and fiscal policy in 1983–84, let the exchange rate depreciate in real terms, and accelerated the pace of structural reform. By 1984, it had met its objectives of inflation reduction and fiscal stabilization and had reduced the current-account deficit to less than 2 percent of GDP. Investment and economic growth remained strong during these years, in contrast to the experience of other highly indebted countries after the debt crisis, and savings increased, thanks to a rebound in household saving.

The second half of the 1980s saw more favorable external developments, such as the fall in the price of oil and the depreciation of the dollar and, up to 1986, a more flexible exchange-rate policy characterized by a large real depreciation. The current-account balance shifted to substantial surpluses, allowing the government to prepay a large portion of the external debt. By 1988, the ratio of foreign debt to GDP was only 20 percent.

What lessons can be drawn from the South Korean experience? Although most of its economic fundamentals were sound (that is, rapid growth driven by investment and exports, and a relatively stable real exchange rate), the situation in 1979–80 was difficult. The policies pursued in the wake of the first oil shock had led to a loosening of monetary policy and to an overvalued real exchange rate, and the second oil price shock and a bout of political turmoil posed a threat to macroeconomic stability. South Korea was able to implement a timely policy adjustment, however, and to recover rapidly after the recession of 1980. Its recovery was facilitated by the continuation of capital inflows, which allowed it to continue borrowing on international capital markets until growth was solidly under way again. Indeed, the ratio of debt to GDP continued to rise until 1982. Once inflation was under control, moreover, and the macroeconomic environment was more stable, the government undertook a second stage of the adjustment process, which was characterized by monetary and fiscal tightening and a gradual real depreciation of the exchange rate. These measures rapidly reduced external imbalances while maintaining strong economic growth.

7 COMPARATIVE ANALYSIS

The country episodes discussed above show both similarities and differences. In this chapter, we examine the intensity of the external shocks affecting the respective countries, using information on the evolution of the terms of trade and of the real rate of interest on external debt (Table 1). We then review the country episodes in view of the sustainability indicators discussed in Chapter 5. A comparison across countries is complicated by two factors. First, the measured intensity of external shocks depends crucially on the length of the period examined before and after the "turning point," and second, the episodes refer to several different periods. For most countries, therefore, we provide two possible breakdowns of the periods for which we calculate our measures of external shocks.

Table 1 highlights the very large increases of real interest rates in Chile, Malaysia, Mexico, and South Korea at about the time of the 1982 debt crisis.[1] The overall impact of the increase in the real interest rate depends on the debt-to-GDP ratio. Among the countries in our sample, Chile and South Korea had a higher ratio of external debt to GDP than Malaysia and Mexico had at the time of the crisis (Table 2). A different breakdown of the period for South Korea and Malaysia shows a much smaller real-interest-rate shock. For Malaysia in particular, this reflects the fact that the policy shift occurred later, when world real interest rates were easing. In Ireland and Israel, real-interest-rate shocks had no significant role at the time of the policy shift, although the increase in world real interest rates at the beginning of the 1980s contributed to the rapid buildup of fiscal imbalances. The 1990s have had more moderate interest-rate changes than the early 1980s had. The impact of variations in U.S. interest rates on capital flows to developing countries in the 1990s has, however, been significant.

With regard to the terms of trade, Chile, Malaysia, Mexico, and South Korea all experienced large shocks, but with different timing. Mexico showed a dramatic improvement in its terms of trade from 1979 to 1981, following the oil-price boom, but a large subsequent

---

[1] The real rate of interest is calculated as the average interest rate on external debt (in U.S. dollars), deflated by a three-year moving average of dollar prices of tradable goods. Tradable goods' prices are proxied by the average of the export price deflator for the country and the industrial country's export price deflator, as in Sachs (1985).

TABLE 1
TERMS OF TRADE AND REAL INTEREST RATES

	Australia	Chile	Ireland	Israel	Malaysia I	Malaysia II	Mexico I	Mexico II	South Korea
	1981–94	1979–81 (1982–83)	1979–86 (1987–90)	1982–84 (1985–86)	1979–84 (1985–86)	1991–94	1977–81 (1982–83)	1991–94 (1995)	1977–82 (1983–88)
Terms of trade	97.0	89.9 (79.0)	97.2 (100.1)	99.6 (95.9)	105.0 (89.6)	97.0	128.7 (103.3)	93.3 (91.4)	99.6 (96.4)
Real interest rate	NA	2.3 (18.8)	NA	NA	4.6 (6.8)	2.3	–9.6 (14.5)	3.4 (NA)	1.1 (5.5)

	Chile	Malaysia I	Mexico I	South Korea
	1979–81 (1982–84)	1979–81 (1982–84)	1979–81 (1982–84)	1979–81 (1982–84)
Terms of trade	89.9 (77.4)	108.3 (101.6)	141.7 (103.3)	96.4 (95.5)
Real interest rate	2.3 (17.8)	–0.5 (9.8)	–9.9 (14.3)	1.4 (12.5)

SOURCES: IMF, *World Economic Outlook* (terms of trade); World Bank, *World Debt Tables*, and IMF, *World Economic Outlook* (real interest rates).

NOTE: The terms of trade is the period average (1970–1995 = 100). The real interest rate is the period average of the interest rate (US$) on external debt, deflated by a three-year moving average of the price inflation of tradables (defined as the average of the increase in the unit values of the country's exports and the increase in the unit value of world exports).

TABLE 2

NINE INDICATORS OF CURRENT-ACCOUNT SUSTAINABILITY

	Australia	Chile		Ireland		Israel		Malaysia I		Malaysia II	Mexico I		Mexico II		South Korea	
	1981–94	1979–81	(1982–83)	1979–86	(1987–90)	1982–84	(1985–86)	1979–84	(1985–86)	1991–94	1977–81	(1982–83)	1991–94	(1995)	1977–82	(1983–88)
Current-account balance	-4.9	-9.1	(7.6)	-8.5	(-0.6)	-7.0	(3.0)	-8.2	(-1.1)	-5.7	-5.0	(0.3)	-0.7	(-0.3)	-5.4	(2.6)
National savings	18.3	7.4	(5.9)	16.0	(15.7)	15.0	(21.0)	26.6	(25.7)	30.0	18.7	(22.0)	15.7	(17.9)	25.6	(31.6)
Investment	23.2	17.0	(13.5)	24.5	(16.3)	22.0	(18.0)	34.8	(26.8)	35.7	23.7	(21.8)	22.4	(18.2)	31.0	(29.0)
Exports	17.0	19.7	(21.3)	52.4	(60.0)	38.0	(41.5)	53.2	(55.6)	82.4	10.6	(17.2)	12.7	(24.0)	32.5	(36.9)
Fiscal balance	-2.2	2.1	(-3.3)	-11.8	(-3.5)	-13.0	(2.0)	-14.5	(-8.9)	-1.5	-8.0	(-11.2)	0.4	(0.0)	-2.8	(0.0)
Growth rate	3.0	7.2	(-7.4)	2.8	(5.7)	2.0	(4.0)	6.9	(0.0)	8.4	7.5	(-2.4)	2.6	(-6.9)	5.8	(10.7)
Real effective exchange rate [a]	93.4	124.1	(118.5)	101.2	(105.9)	99.2	(93.1)	117.9	(111.8)	83.5	126.4	(103.5)	113.9	(76.0)	103.6	(92.2)
Interest payments	2.1	5.5	(8.6)	3.7	(2.7)	4.0	(5.8)	4.4	(5.4)	2.0	3.9	(6.7)	2.2	(NA)	5.6	(1.7)
Gross external debt [b]	36.0	48.2	(89.5)	50.0	(32.7)	46.0	(45.0)	55.2	(78.9)	35.1	31.4	(62.7)	35.5	(65.1)	50.0	(19.6)

SOURCES: IMF, *International Finance Statistics*; World Bank, *World Debt Tables*, and national sources.

NOTE: The current-account balance, savings, investment, exports of goods and services, and fiscal balance are average ratios of GDP for the period. The growth rate and CPI-based real effective exchange rate are period averages. Interest payments and gross external debt are ratios of GDP for the last year of the period.

[a] Average of 1970–95 = 100.

[b] For Australia and Israel, net external debt.

deterioration, which brought levels back to those of the late 1970s. South Korea was hit heavily by the oil shock, with a large terms-of-trade deterioration in 1980. Chile's terms of trade worsened considerably from 1980 onward, and Malaysia's adjustment period in 1985–86 also coincided with a large negative terms-of-trade shock. The overall effect of a terms-of-trade shock depends on the share of exports and imports in GDP. Among the countries in our sample, Chile and Mexico had a lower share of exports in GDP than South Korea and Malaysia had (Table 2). None of the other episodes considered were characterized by large fluctuations in the terms of trade.

The comparison of country experiences shows that large terms-of-trade and real-interest-rate shocks were confined to four episodes at about the time of the debt crisis. Among these four, Malaysia and South Korea were able to withstand shocks without suffering external crises, whereas Chile and Mexico were not. The nonconclusive nature of our findings in this regard is confirmed by more comprehensive studies of heavily indebted countries before and after the debt crisis (see Cline, 1995, for a recent survey). These studies have found that the intensity of external shocks is not a clear-cut indicator of future difficulties in servicing debt.

We now turn to the indicators of sustainability discussed in Chapter 5. Tables 2 and 3 summarize the indicators for the various country episodes. The main lesson to be drawn from these episodes is that it is necessary to consider a combination of factors, rather than single variables, in gauging whether persistent imbalances will be sustainable.

A first factor is the ratio of external debt to GDP. This ratio, however, does not allow for discrimination in our sample between crisis and noncrisis episodes. Indeed, ratios of external debt to GDP were much higher in Ireland, Israel, Malaysia I, and South Korea than in Mexico in either 1981 or 1994.

A second factor is the interest burden of external debt. This factor does not help to discriminate clearly between crisis and noncrisis episodes. It singles out the experiences of the 1980s, and in particular those of Chile and South Korea, but for the 1990s shows little difference across countries. The "operational solvency condition" (equation 5) implies that the perpetual resource transfer needed to prevent the ratio of external debt to GDP from increasing is determined by the interest burden adjusted for growth and changes in the real exchange rate. In Chile and Mexico I, all three components turned unfavorable in the run-up to the crisis. Interest rates increased, high growth came to a halt, and the real exchange rate began to depreciate. In Malaysia and South Korea, similar elements were at work, but the slowdown in growth was short-lived. In Ireland and Israel, the interest burden prior to the policy shift was as high as in Mexico I before the debt crisis, but growth accelerated following stabilization, and there was no substantial depreciation in the real exchange rate. In the case of Mexico II, the crisis was preceded by a relatively modest increase in the interest burden but was followed by a large real depreciation and a deep recession. Based on our sample, it therefore appears that the resource transfer, although clearly a measure of the cost of external adjustment, is not an unambiguous predictor *ex ante*.

A third factor is the ratio of exports to GDP (Table 2). Countries such as Ireland, Israel, South Korea, and Malaysia, which successfully adjusted after experiencing large current-account imbalances, had a large export share. Chile and Mexico (especially in 1982), by contrast, showed a lower ratio of exports to GDP—although it should be noted that exports were rising rapidly prior to all three of the crises considered (Chile and Mexico I and II). This finding coincides with results presented in Sachs (1985), who compares East Asian and Latin American countries at the time of the 1982 debt crisis.[2] The episodes we consider thus suggest that large current-account imbalances are less likely to lead to external crises when the economy has a large export base. Indeed, the interest burden and the level of external debt appear to be better indicators of sustainability when expressed as ratios to exports, rather than as ratios to GDP.

A fourth factor is the real exchange rate. It is notoriously difficult to determine an appropriate benchmark against which to measure any misalignment in the real exchange rate. In Table 2, we report the level of the real effective exchange rate (measured in terms of relative trade-weighted consumer price indices) relative to historical averages. The three crisis episodes considered are all characterized by a sustained appreciation of the real exchange rate in the period preceding the crisis, leading to an appreciated level of that rate with respect to historical averages. Malaysia (in the early 1980s) and South Korea (prior to 1980) also experienced a sustained real appreciation. It is interesting to note that an exchange-rate devaluation was undertaken by all the countries in our sample that had fixed or managed exchange-rate regimes. For some, it was forced by events; for others, it was preventive. Australia is the only country in our sample with a flexible exchange rate, and along

[2] Australia is an outlier in this respect, having a relatively low export share. It also has a much higher GDP per capita than any of the other countries in our sample.

with Malaysia in the 1990s, it shows a relatively depreciated real exchange rate with respect to historical averages during the period of large current-account deficits. Our sample thus suggests that large current-account imbalances are more likely to result in a crisis when they are accompanied by a relatively appreciated level of the real exchange rate.

A fifth factor is the level of national savings and investment (Table 2). These were extremely low in Chile in the run-up to the 1982 crisis, whereas both Malaysia and South Korea had high savings and investment rates. Savings were also low in Mexico in the early 1990s, as they were in Ireland and Israel. It is noteworthy that in both Chile and Mexico II, the low savings rates were attributable to low private savings, rather than to public-sector imbalances, but that in Ireland and Israel, low savings rates were associated with large public-sector imbalances. All three crisis episodes, Chile, Mexico I, and Mexico II, are thus characterized by low savings, especially by the standards of middle-income developing countries. It should be noted, however, that other countries in our sample with low savings were able to avoid external crises (for recent cross-sectional studies of the determinants of savings, see Masson, Bayoumi, and Samiei, 1995, and Edwards, 1995).

A sixth factor is the fiscal balance (Table 2). The evidence from our sample suggests that the absence of large fiscal imbalances *ex ante* does not imply that current-account deficits will prove sustainable. Chile and Mexico II are cases in point.[3] Clearly, large fiscal imbalances, which were present in Ireland, Israel, Malaysia I, and Mexico I, raise issues of fiscal sustainability and would, therefore, require a policy shift. Indeed, the main element of the policy reversals in Ireland, Israel, and Malaysia I consisted in the drastic reduction of the fiscal deficit.

The striking changes in the composition of capital flows to developing countries between the late 1970s–early 1980s and the early 1990s makes it difficult to compare episodes occurring in different decades. This limits our ability, already constrained by the small size of our sample, to relate financial and capital-account indicators to current-account sustainability. Table 3 nevertheless reports some summary statistics on the level and composition of external liabilities and capital flows.

Among these statistics, the cumulative value of current-account imbalances as a fraction of GDP can be taken as an approximate

---

[3] It should be noted that all the external crises we considered entailed, *ex post*, a large fiscal cost for the government in the form of bailouts of banks and firms as well as in the assumption by the budget of private external debt.

TABLE 3

SIX INDICATORS OF CURRENT-ACCOUNT SUSTAINABILITY

	Australia	Chile	Ireland	Israel	Malaysia I	Malaysia II	Mexico I	Mexico II	South Korea
	1981–94	1979–81 (1982–83)	1979–86 (1987–90)	1982–84 (1985–86)	1979–84 (1985–86)	1991–94	1977–81 (1982–83)	1991–94 (1995)	1977–82 (1983–88)
Net external debt[a]	36.0	36.2 (88.8)	35.7 (22.8)	46.0 (45.0)	42.1 (53.8)	-2.2	29.5 (59.5)	32.3 (58.3)	44.5 (12.8)
Cumulative current-account deficits[b]	54.8	44.2 (83.7)	62.1 (37.4)	43.2 (41.2)	31.3 (43.5)	32.0	26.0 (42.3)	41.3 (62.8)	33.9 (0.5)
Short-term debt	24.0	19.3 (14.5)	NA	NA	13.5 (13.2)	25.0	32.0 (11.0)	24.6 (NA)	33.2 (30.0)
Foreign-exchange reserves	9.2	24.8 (14.6)	22.2 (33.0)	25.5 (34.6)	23.7 (31.7)	106.3	6.4 (5.2)	5.0 (10.4)	7.9 (34.9)
Net portfolio flows	1.4	0.0 (0.0)	3.0 (0.9)	1.1 (1.4)	0.0 (0.0)	2.2	0.0 (0.0)	4.9 (-4.3)	0.0 (0.1)
Net FDI flows	0.7	0.9 (1.3)	1.0 (0.3)	-0.2 (0.2)	4.1 (2.1)	7.9	0.9 (0.7)	1.8 (2.8)	0.1 (0.3)

SOURCES: IMF, *International Finance Statistics*; World Bank, *World Debt Tables*; OECD, *Economic Surveys*; national sources.
NOTE: Net external debt and cumulative current-account deficits are ratios to GDP for the last year of the period. Short-term debt and foreign-exchange reserves are ratios to total debt for the last year of the period. Portfolio and FDI flows are ratios to GDP for the period average.
[a] External debt minus nongold foreign-exchange reserves.
[b] Initial net external debt plus cumulative value of current-account deficits, as a ratio of end-of-period GDP.

measure of net external liabilities. For Australia, Ireland, Malaysia II, and Mexico II, this measure exceeds the ratio of external debt to GDP net of foreign-exchange reserves. This would be expected, given the importance in these episodes of non-debt-creating capital inflows such as foreign direct investment. For Mexico I, the measure of net external liabilities is well below net external debt, especially in 1982–83, because of capital flight. For Chile and Israel, the gap between the two measures is rather small.

As our discussion also emphasizes, other factors of debt composition, such as the proportion of short-term debt in total debt, can potentially play a role in determining the sustainability of external imbalances. The data do not, however, show a consistent pattern in this respect (Table 3). In Chile, for example, the share of short-term debt was considerably lower (19 percent) just before the debt crisis than it was in Mexico and South Korea (above 30 percent). In countries such as Australia and Ireland, which have more-developed bond markets, a significant fraction of external debt is denominated in domestic currency, a factor that shields these countries from changes in the real exchange rate. Table 3 also presents data on net foreign direct investment and portfolio flows. Because these flows became significant for most countries only in the 1990s, it is impossible to draw inferences from the limited sample of episodes we consider.

The quality of financial intermediation, and especially the fragility of the banking system, is also emphasized in the theoretical literature. This element is difficult to quantify and is therefore not included in our tables, but it played an important role in all the crises we considered.[4] Weaknesses in the supervision of the banking system, distortions in the incentive structure of banks, the practice of directed bank lending, and lack of competition within the banking sector and with nonbank financial institutions imply inefficiencies in the intermediation of the external funds that finance large current-account deficits. For a given size of current-account imbalances, these inefficiencies make the economy more vulnerable to changes in the sentiments of foreign investors, as well as to other shocks.

The degree of political instability and policy uncertainty is also difficult to quantify. Policy uncertainty played a role in the two Mexican crises. Signs of a possible crisis were already surfacing in 1982 and

[4] For a recent attempt to relate balance-of-payments and banking crises, see Kaminsky and Reinhart (1996). Goldstein (1996) provides a discussion of potential indicators of financial crises that shares many features with the present study.

1994, but the imminence of an election made the government reluctant to undertake severe adjustment measures. In South Korea, the 1980 recession was probably accentuated by the difficult political situation following the assassination of President Park. In Israel, 1984 was an election year, during which a loose economic-policy stance led to an increasing fiscal deficit and further acceleration of inflation; the successful adjustment in 1985 was undertaken by a "national unity" government. In Ireland, the fiscal adjustment in 1982 was made more difficult by instability in the governing coalition. Interestingly, however, the successful adjustment of 1987 was undertaken by a minority government—albeit with general political support. Only in Chile and Malaysia did political instability fail to play a role.

8   CONCLUSIONS

Persistent current-account imbalances are often viewed as a sign of weakness that implies a need for policy action. Economic theory suggests, however, that intertemporal borrowing and lending are natural vehicles for achieving faster capital accumulation, a more efficient allocation of investment, and the smoothing of consumption. In this study, we have considered to what degree persistent current-account imbalances can be taken as a sign of a probable "hard landing," or crisis, ahead. We have argued that traditional measures of sustainability, based solely on the notion of intertemporal solvency, may not always be appropriate, because they sidestep the issue of a country's willingness to repay its external obligations and the related issue of the willingness of foreign investors to continue lending on current terms. We have therefore proposed an alternative notion of sustainability that emphasizes the willingness to pay and to lend in addition to simple solvency.

Based on theoretical considerations, we have examined a list of indicators that may shed light on the sustainability of external imbalances. We have investigated the role of these indicators in the experiences of a number of countries that have run persistent current-account imbalances—some of which have experienced external crises. From these episodes, we have distilled a number of implications regarding the sustainability of external imbalances. We conclude that a specific threshold on persistent current-account deficits (such as 5 percent of GDP for three to four years) is not in itself a sufficiently informative indicator of sustainability. The size of current-account imbalances should instead be considered in conjunction with exchange-rate policy and structural factors such as the degree of openness, the levels of saving and investment, and the health of the financial system. Measures of the external burden, such as external debt and debt interest, provide a better indicator of sustainability when they are expressed as a fraction of exports than as a fraction of GDP.

Future research, combining a more comprehensive set of episodes, might profitably rely on formal econometric analysis to gauge the relative importance of these indicators of sustainability. One possible strategy would be to characterize "turning points" in trade and current-account imbalances and to examine which indicators can predict whether these shifts occur smoothly or whether they are associated with a structural break in consumption and economic activity. Such a break is more likely to occur when shifts are forced by events (a sudden reversal of capital flows, for example) that leave the country with severe difficulties in servicing outstanding external obligations.

REFERENCES

Aghevli, Bijan, and Jorge Márquez-Ruarte, "A Case of Successful Adjustment: Korea's Experience During 1980–84," Occasional Paper No. 39, Washington, D.C., International Monetary Fund, August 1985.

Alesina, Alberto, Sule Özler, Nouriel Roubini, and Phillip Swagel, "Political Instability and Growth," *Journal of Economic Growth*, 1 (June 1996), pp. 189–211.

Alesina, Alberto, and Guido Tabellini, "External Debt, Capital Flight and Political Risk," *Journal of International Economics*, 27 (November 1989), pp. 199–220.

———, "A Positive Theory of Fiscal Deficits and Government Debt in a Democracy," *Review of Economic Studies*, 57 (July 1990), pp. 403–414.

Asea, Patrick K., and Enrique G. Mendoza, "The Balassa-Samuelson Model: A General Equilibrium Appraisal," *Review of International Economics*, 2 (October 1994), pp. 244–267.

Barro, Robert J., "Are Government Bonds Net Wealth?" *Journal of Political Economy*, 82 (November 1974), pp. 1095–1117.

Barro, Robert J., and Xavier Sala-i-Martin, "World Real Interest Rates," *NBER Macroeconomics Annual*, Cambridge, Mass., MIT Press, 1990, pp. 16–59.

Bartolini, Leonardo, and Allan Drazen, "Capital Controls as a Signal," *American Economic Review* (forthcoming 1996).

Bevilaqua, Alfonso S., "Dual Resource Transfers and the Secondary Market Price of Developing Countries' External Debt," Discussion Paper No. 344, Pontifícia Universidade Católica, Rio de Janeiro, December 1995.

Bruno, Michael, *Crisis, Stabilization and Economic Reform: Therapy by Consensus*, Oxford, Clarendon; New York, Oxford University Press, 1993.

Buffie, Edward F., "Economic Policy and Foreign Debt in Mexico," in Jeffrey Sachs, ed., *Developing Country Debt and Economic Performance*, Vol. 2, Chicago, University of Chicago Press for National Bureau of Economic Research, 1989, pp. 395–551.

Bufman, Gil, and Leonardo Leiderman, "Israel's Stabilization: Some Important Policy Lessons," in Sebastian Edwards and Rudiger Dornbusch, eds., *Reform, Recovery and Growth*, Chicago, University of Chicago Press for National Bureau of Economic Research, 1995, pp. 177–215.

Calvo, Guillermo A., "Temporary Stabilization: Predetermined Exchange Rates," *Journal of Political Economy*, 94 (December 1986), pp. 1319–1329.

———, "Servicing the Public Debt: The Role of Expectations," *American Economic Review*, 78 (September 1988), pp. 647–661.

———, "Varieties of Capital Market Crises," University of Maryland, Department of Economics, February 1995, processed.

Calvo, Guillermo A., Leonardo Leiderman, and Carmen M. Reinhart "Capital Inflows and Real Exchange Rate Appreciation in Latin America: The Role of External Factors," *International Monetary Fund Staff Papers*, 40 (March 1993), pp. 108–151.

———, "The Capital Inflow Problem: Concepts and Issues," *Contemporary Economic Policy*, 12 (July 1994), pp. 54–66.

Calvo, Guillermo A., and Enrique G. Mendoza, "Mexico's Balance-of-Payments Crisis: A Chronicle of a Death Foretold," *Journal of International Economics*, 41 (November 1996a), pp. 235–264.

———, "On the Costs and Benefits of International Diversification and Volatile Capital Flows," University of Maryland, Department of Economics, and Federal Reserve Board, June 1996b, processed.

Claessens, Stijn, Michael Dooley, and Andrew Warner, "Portfolio Flows: Hot or Cold?" *World Bank Economic Review*, 9 (January 1995), pp. 153–174.

Cline, William R., *International Debt Reexamined*, Washington, D.C., Institute for International Economics, 1995.

Coe, David, and Elhanan Helpman, "International R&D Spillovers," *European Economic Review*, 39 (May 1995), pp. 859–887.

Coe, David, Elhanan Helpman, and Alex Hoffmaister, "North-South R&D Spillovers," International Monetary Fund Working Paper No. 94/144, Washington, D.C., International Monetary Fund, December 1994.

Cohen, Daniel, "The Debt Crisis: A Postmortem," *NBER Macroeconomics Annual*, Cambridge, Mass., MIT Press, 1992, pp. 65–105.

———, "The Sustainability of African Debt," Paris, Centre pour La Recherche Economique et Mathématique Appliquée, September 1995, processed.

Cole, Harold L., and Timothy J. Kehoe, "A Self-Fulfilling Model of Mexico's 1994–1995 Debt Crises," *Journal of International Economics*, 41 (November 1996), pp. 309–330.

Collins, Susan M., and Won-Am Park, "External Debt and Macroeconomic Performance in South Korea," in Jeffrey Sachs, ed., *Developing Country Debt and Economic Performance*, Vol. 3, Chicago, University of Chicago Press for National Bureau of Economic Research, 1989, pp. 153–369.

Corbo, Vittorio, and Stanley Fischer, "Lessons from the Chilean Stabilization and Recovery," in Barry P. Bosworth, Rudiger Dornbusch, and Raúl Labán, eds., *The Chilean Economy: Policy Lessons and Challenges*, Washington, D.C., Brookings Institution, 1994, pp. 29–80.

Corden, W. Max, "Does the Current Account Matter? The Old View and the New," *Economic Papers*, 10 (September 1991), pp. 1–19.

Corsetti, Giancarlo, and Nouriel Roubini, "Fiscal Deficits, Public Debt and Government Solvency: Evidence from OECD Countries," *Journal of the Japanese and International Economies*, 5 (December 1991), pp. 354–380.

Cukierman, Alex, Sebastian Edwards, and Guido Tabellini, "Seigniorage and Political Instability," *American Economic Review*, 82 (June 1992), pp. 537–555.

de la Cuadra, Sergio, and Salvador Valdes-Prieto, "Myths and Facts about Financial Liberalization in Chile: 1974-83," in Philip Brock, ed., *If Texas Were Chile: A Primer on Banking Reform*, San Francisco, ICS Press, 1992, pp. 11–101.

Demery, David, and Lionel Demery, *Adjustment and Equity in Malaysia*, Paris, Organisation for Economic Co-operation and Development, 1992.

Diamond, Douglas, and Philip Dybvig, "Bank Runs, Deposit Insurance, and Liquidity," *Journal of Political Economy*, 91 (June 1983), pp. 401–419.

Diaz-Alejandro, Carlos F., "Latin American Debt: I Don't Think We Are in Kansas Anymore," *Brookings Papers on Economic Activity*, 1 (1984), pp. 335–389.

———, "Goodbye Financial Repression, Hello Financial Crash," *Journal of Development Economics*, 19 (September/October 1985), pp. 1–24.

Dooley, Michael P., "A Retrospective on the Debt Crisis," in Peter B. Kenen, ed., *Understanding Interdependence: The Macroeconomics of the Open Economy*, Princeton, N.J, Princeton University Press, 1995, pp. 262–288.

Dornbusch, Rudiger, "Credibility, Debt and Unemployment: Ireland's Failed Stabilization," *Economic Policy*, 8 (April 1989), pp. 173–210.

———, "The New Classical Macroeconomics and Stabilization Policy," *American Economic Review Papers and Proceedings*, 80 (May 1990), pp. 143–147.

Dornbusch, Rudiger, Ilan Goldfajn, and Rodrigo Valdes, "Currency Crises and Collapses," *Brookings Papers on Economic Activity*, 2 (1995), pp. 219–293.

Dornbusch, Rudiger, and Alejandro Werner, "Mexico: Stabilization, Reform and No Growth," *Brookings Papers on Economic Activity*, 1 (1994), pp. 253–315.

Eaton, Jonathan, and Raquel Fernández, "Sovereign Debt," in Gene M. Grossman and Kenneth S. Rogoff, eds., *Handbook of International Economics*, Vol. 3, Amsterdam and New York, North-Holland, Elsevier, 1995, pp. 2031–2077.

Eaton, Jonathan, and Mark Gersovitz, *Poor-Country Borrowing in Private Financial Markets and the Repudiation Issue*, Princeton Studies in International Finance No. 47, Princeton, N.J., Princeton University, International Finance Section, June 1981.

Edwards, Sebastian, *Real Exchange Rates, Devaluation and Adjustment*, Cambridge, Mass., MIT Press, 1989.

———, "Why Are Savings Rates So Different Across Countries? An International Comparative Analysis," National Bureau of Economic Research Working Paper No. 5097, Cambridge, Mass., National Bureau of Economic Research, April 1995.

Edwards, Sebastian, and Alejandra Cox-Edwards, *Monetarism and Liberalization: The Chilean Experiment*, Cambridge, Mass., MIT Press, 1987.

Engel, Charles, "Real Exchange Rates and Relative Prices: An Empirical Investigation," *Journal of Monetary Economics*, 32 (August 1993), pp. 35–50.

————, "Long-Run PPP May Not Hold After All," National Bureau of Economic Research Working Paper No. 5646, Cambridge, Mass., National Bureau of Economic Research, July 1996.

Fernández-Arias, Eduardo, and Peter Montiel, "The Surge in Capital Inflows to Developing Countries: An Analytical Overview," *World Bank Economic Review*, 10 (January 1996), pp. 51–77.

Flood, Robert, and Peter Garber, "Collapsing Exchange-Rate Regimes: Some Linear Examples," *Journal of International Economics*, 17 (August 1984), pp. 1–13.

Folkerts-Landau, David, "The Changing Role of International Bank Lending in Development Finance," *International Monetary Fund Staff Papers*, 32 (June 1985), pp. 317–363.

Frenkel, Jacob, Assaf Razin, and Chi-Wa Yuen, *Fiscal Policy and Growth in the World Economy*, 3rd rev. ed., Cambridge, Mass., MIT Press, 1996.

Fry, Maxwell, "Saving, Investment and Current Account Balance: A Malaysian and East Asian Perspective," International Finance Group Working Paper 93–05, University of Birmingham, June 1993.

Gale, David, "Pure Exchange Equilibrium of Dynamic Models," *Journal of Economic Theory*, 6 (February 1973), pp. 12-36.

Gertler, Mark, and Kenneth S. Rogoff, "North-South Lending and Endogenous Domestic Capital Market Inefficiencies," *Journal of Monetary Economics*, 26 (October 1990), pp. 245–266.

Ghosh, Atish R., and Jonathan D. Ostry, "Export Instability and the External Balance in Developing Countries," *International Monetary Fund Staff Papers*, 41 (June 1994), pp. 214–235.

————, "The Current Account in Developing Countries: A Perspective from the Consumption Smoothing Approach," *World Bank Economic Review*, 9 (May 1995), pp. 305–333.

Giavazzi, Francesco, and Marco Pagano, "Can Fiscal Contractions Be Expansionary? Tales of Two Small European Countries," *NBER Macroeconomics Annual*, Cambridge, Mass., MIT Press, 1990, pp. 75–110.

Glick, Reuven, and Kenneth S. Rogoff, "Global versus Country-Specific Productivity Shocks and the Current Account," *Journal of Monetary Economics*, 35 (April 1995), pp. 159–192.

Goldstein, Morris, "Presumptive Indicators/Early Warning Signals of Vulnerability to Financial Crises in Emerging-Market Economies," Washington, D.C., Institute for International Economics, January 1996, processed.

Grilli, Vittorio, and Gian Maria Milesi-Ferretti, "Economic Effects and Structural Determinants of Capital Controls," *International Monetary Fund Staff Papers*, 42 (September 1995), pp. 517–551.

Haggard, Stephen, Richard Cooper, Susan M. Collins, Chongsoo Kim, and Sung-Tael Ro, *Macroeconomic Policy and Adjustment in Korea, 1970-1990*, Cambridge, Mass., Harvard Institute for International Development, 1994.

Horne, Jocelyn, "Criteria of External Sustainability," *European Economic Review*, 35 (December 1991), pp. 1559–1574.

International Monetary Fund (IMF), *International Capital Markets: Developments, Prospects and Policy Issues*, Washington, D.C., International Monetary Fund, 1995a.

———, *International Financial Statistics*, Washington, D.C., International Monetary Fund, various years.

———, *World Economic Outlook*, Washington, D.C., International Monetary Fund, May 1995b.

Jappelli, Tullio, and Marco Pagano, "Savings, Growth, and Liquidity Constraints," *Quarterly Journal of Economics*, 109 (February 1994), pp. 83–109.

Kaminsky, Graciela, and Carmen M. Reinhart, "The Twin Crises: The Causes of Banking of Balance-of-Payments Problems," International Finance Discussion Paper No. 544, Washington, D.C., Board of Governors of the Federal Reserve System, March 1996.

Krugman, Paul, "A Model of Balance-of-Payments Crises," *Journal of Money, Credit and Banking*, 11 (August 1979), pp. 311–325.

———, "Is the Strong Dollar Sustainable," in *The US Dollar—Recent Developments, Outlook and Policy Options*, Kansas City, Mo., Federal Reserve Bank of Kansas City, 1985, pp. 103–132.

Leiderman, Leonardo, and Assaf Razin, "Determinants of External Imbalances: The Role of Taxes, Government Spending, and Productivity," *Journal of the Japanese and International Economies*, 5 (December 1991), pp. 421–450.

Masson, Paul R., Tamim Bayoumi, and Hossein S. Samiei, "International Evidence on the Determinants of Private Savings," in *Staff Studies for the World Economic Outlook*, Washington, D.C., International Monetary Fund, 1995, pp. 1–22.

Mendoza, Enrique G., "Terms of Trade Uncertainty and Economic Growth: Are Risk Indicators Significant in Growth Regressions," *Journal of Development Economics* (forthcoming 1996).

Milesi-Ferretti, Gian Maria, "The Disadvantage of Tying Their Hands," *Economic Journal*, 105 (November 1995), pp. 1381–1402.

———, "A Simple Model of Disinflation and the Optimality of Doing Nothing," *European Economic Review*, 39 (August 1995), pp. 1385–1404.

Obstfeld, Maurice, "A Model of Balance of Payments Crises," *American Economic Review*, 76 (March 1986), pp. 72–81.

———, "The Logic of Currency Crises," *Cahiers Economiques et Monétaires* (Banque de France), 43 (1994), pp. 189–213.

———, "Models of Currency Crises with Self-Fulfilling Features," *European Economic Review*, 40 (April 1996), pp. 1037–1047.

Obstfeld, Maurice, and Kenneth S. Rogoff, *Foundations of International Macroeconomics*, Cambridge, Mass., MIT Press, 1996.

Organisation for Economic Co-operation and Development (OECD), *Economic Surveys: Australia*, Paris, Organisation for Economic Co-operation and Development, various years.

———, *Economic Surveys: Ireland*, Paris, Organisation for Economic Co-operation and Development, 1993 and other years.

Pitchford, John, *Australia's Foreign Debt: Myths and Realities*, Allen and Unwin, 1989.

Razin, Assaf, "The Dynamic-Optimizing Approach to the Current Account: Theory and Evidence," in Peter B. Kenen, ed., *Understanding Interdependence: The Macroeconomics of the Open Economy*, Princeton, N.J., Princeton University Press, 1995, pp. 169–198.

Razin, Assaf, and Efraim Sadka, "Fiscal Balance During Inflation, Disinflation and Immigration: Policy Lessons," *Swedish Economic Policy Review* (forthcoming 1996).

Razin, Assaf, Efraim Sadka, and Chi-Wa Yuen, "A Pecking Order Theory of Capital Inflows and International Tax Principles," International Monetary Fund Working Paper No. 96/26, Washington, D.C., International Monetary Fund, April 1996.

Rojas-Suarez, Liliana, and Steven Weisbrod, "Financial Fragilities in Latin America: The 1980s and the 1990s," Occasional Paper No. 132, Washington, D.C., International Monetary Fund, October 1995.

Sachs, Jeffrey, "The Current Account and Macroeconomic Adjustment in the 1970s, *Brookings Papers on Economic Activity*, 1 (1981), pp. 201–268.

——, "The Current Account in the Macroeconomic Adjustment Process," *Scandinavian Journal of Economics*, 84 (No. 2, 1982), pp. 147–159.

——, "External Debt and Macroeconomic Performance in Latin America and East Asia," *Brookings Papers on Economic Activity*, 1 (1985), pp. 523–564.

Sachs, Jeffrey, Aaron Tornell, and Andrés Velasco, "The Collapse of the Mexican Peso: What Have We Learned?" *Economic Policy*, 22 (April 1996), pp. 15–63.

Sachs, Jeffrey, and Andrew Warner, "Economic Reform and the Process of Global Integration," *Brookings Papers on Economic Activity*, 1 (1995), pp. 1–95.

SaKong, Il, *Korea in the World Economy*, Washington, D.C., Institute for International Economics, 1993.

Sheffrin, Steven, and Wing Thye Woo, "Present Value Tests of an Intertemporal Model of the Current Account," *Journal of International Economics*, 29 (November 1990), pp. 237–253.

Soon, Cho, "The Dynamics of Korean Economic Development," Washington, D.C., Institute for International Economics, 1993.

Stiglitz, Joseph, and Andrew Weiss, "Credit Rationing in Models with Imperfect Information," *American Economic Review*, 71 (June 1981), pp. 393–410.

Sutherland, Alan, "Fiscal Crises and Demand: Can High Public Debt Reverse the Effects of Fiscal Policy?" CEPR Discussion Paper No. 1246, London, Centre for Economic Policy Research, September 1995.

Velasco, Andrés, "Liberalization, Crisis, Intervention: The Chilean Financial System, 1975–85," in Tomás J. T. Baliño and V. Sundararajan, eds., *Banking Crises: Cases and Issues*, Washington, D.C., International Monetary Fund, 1991, pp. 113–174.

Walsh, Brendan, "The Real Exchange Rate, Fiscal Policy and the Current Account: Interpreting Recent Irish Experience," Working Paper No. 96/10, University College, Dublin, March 1996.

Williamson, John, "Comments on Sachs," *Brookings Papers on Economic Activity*, 1 (1985), pp. 565–570.

World Bank, *World Debt Tables*, Washington, D.C., World Bank, various years.

PUBLICATIONS OF THE
INTERNATIONAL FINANCE SECTION

Notice to Contributors

The International Finance Section publishes papers in four series: ESSAYS IN INTERNATIONAL FINANCE, PRINCETON STUDIES IN INTERNATIONAL FINANCE, and SPECIAL PAPERS IN INTERNATIONAL ECONOMICS contain new work not published elsewhere. REPRINTS IN INTERNATIONAL FINANCE reproduce journal articles previously published by Princeton faculty members associated with the Section. The Section welcomes the submission of manuscripts for publication under the following guidelines:

ESSAYS are meant to disseminate new views about international financial matters and should be accessible to well-informed nonspecialists as well as to professional economists. Technical terms, tables, and charts should be used sparingly; mathematics should be avoided.

STUDIES are devoted to new research on international finance, with preference given to empirical work. They should be comparable in originality and technical proficiency to papers published in leading economic journals. They should be of medium length, longer than a journal article but shorter than a book.

SPECIAL PAPERS are surveys of research on particular topics and should be suitable for use in undergraduate courses. They may be concerned with international trade as well as international finance. They should also be of medium length.

Manuscripts should be submitted in triplicate, typed single sided and double spaced throughout on 8½ by 11 white bond paper. Publication can be expedited if manuscripts are computer keyboarded in WordPerfect 5.1 or a compatible program. Additional instructions and a style guide are available from the Section.

How to Obtain Publications

The Section's publications are distributed free of charge to college, university, and public libraries and to nongovernmental, nonprofit research institutions. Eligible institutions may ask to be placed on the Section's permanent mailing list.

Individuals and institutions not qualifying for free distribution may receive all publications for the calendar year for a subscription fee of $40.00. Late subscribers will receive all back issues for the year during which they subscribe. Subscribers should notify the Section promptly of any change in address, giving the old address as well as the new.

Publications may be ordered individually, with payment made in advance. ESSAYS and REPRINTS cost $8.00 each; STUDIES and SPECIAL PAPERS cost $11.00. An additional $1.50 should be sent for postage and handling within the United States, Canada, and Mexico; $1.75 should be added for surface delivery outside the region.

All payments must be made in U.S. dollars. Subscription fees and charges for single issues will be waived for organizations and individuals in countries where foreign-exchange regulations prohibit dollar payments.

Please address all correspondence, submissions, and orders to:

International Finance Section
Department of Economics, Fisher Hall
Princeton University
Princeton, New Jersey 08544-1021

List of Recent Publications

A complete list of publications may be obtained from the International Finance Section.

ESSAYS IN INTERNATIONAL FINANCE

167. Rainer Stefano Masera, *An Increasing Role for the ECU: A Character in Search of a Script.* (June 1987)
168. Paul Mosley, *Conditionality as Bargaining Process: Structural-Adjustment Lending, 1980-86.* (October 1987)
169. Paul A. Volcker, Ralph C. Bryant, Leonhard Gleske, Gottfried Haberler, Alexandre Lamfalussy, Shijuro Ogata, Jesús Silva-Herzog, Ross M. Starr, James Tobin, and Robert Triffin, *International Monetary Cooperation: Essays in Honor of Henry C. Wallich.* (December 1987)
170. Shafiqul Islam, *The Dollar and the Policy-Performance-Confidence Mix.* (July 1988)
171. James M. Boughton, *The Monetary Approach to Exchange Rates: What Now Remains?* (October 1988)
172. Jack M. Guttentag and Richard M. Herring, *Accounting for Losses On Sovereign Debt: Implications for New Lending.* (May 1989)
173. Benjamin J. Cohen, *Developing-Country Debt: A Middle Way.* (May 1989)
174. Jeffrey D. Sachs, *New Approaches to the Latin American Debt Crisis.* (July 1989)
175. C. David Finch, *The IMF: The Record and the Prospect.* (September 1989)
176. Graham Bird, *Loan-Loss Provisions and Third-World Debt.* (November 1989)
177. Ronald Findlay, *The "Triangular Trade" and the Atlantic Economy of the Eighteenth Century: A Simple General-Equilibrium Model.* (March 1990)
178. Alberto Giovannini, *The Transition to European Monetary Union.* (November 1990)
179. Michael L. Mussa, *Exchange Rates in Theory and in Reality.* (December 1990)
180. Warren L. Coats, Jr., Reinhard W. Furstenberg, and Peter Isard, *The SDR System and the Issue of Resource Transfers.* (December 1990)
181. George S. Tavlas, *On the International Use of Currencies: The Case of the Deutsche Mark.* (March 1991)
182. Tommaso Padoa-Schioppa, ed., with Michael Emerson, Kumiharu Shigehara, and Richard Portes, *Europe After 1992: Three Essays.* (May 1991)
183. Michael Bruno, *High Inflation and the Nominal Anchors of an Open Economy.* (June 1991)
184. Jacques J. Polak, *The Changing Nature of IMF Conditionality.* (September 1991)
185. Ethan B. Kapstein, *Supervising International Banks: Origins and Implications of the Basle Accord.* (December 1991)
186. Alessandro Giustiniani, Francesco Papadia, and Daniela Porciani, *Growth and Catch-Up in Central and Eastern Europe: Macroeconomic Effects on Western Countries.* (April 1992)
187. Michele Fratianni, Jürgen von Hagen, and Christopher Waller, *The Maastricht Way to EMU.* (June 1992)
188. Pierre-Richard Agénor, *Parallel Currency Markets in Developing Countries: Theory, Evidence, and Policy Implications.* (November 1992)

189. Beatriz Armendariz de Aghion and John Williamson, *The G-7's Joint-and-Several Blunder*. (April 1993)

190. Paul Krugman, *What Do We Need to Know About the International Monetary System?* (July 1993)

191. Peter M. Garber and Michael G. Spencer, *The Dissolution of the Austro-Hungarian Empire: Lessons for Currency Reform*. (February 1994)

192. Raymond F. Mikesell, *The Bretton Woods Debates: A Memoir*. (March 1994)

193. Graham Bird, *Economic Assistance to Low-Income Countries: Should the Link be Resurrected?* (July 1994)

194. Lorenzo Bini-Smaghi, Tommaso Padoa-Schioppa, and Francesco Papadia, *The Transition to EMU in the Maastricht Treaty*. (November 1994)

195. Ariel Buira, *Reflections on the International Monetary System*. (January 1995)

196. Shinji Takagi, *From Recipient to Donor: Japan's Official Aid Flows, 1945 to 1990 and Beyond*. (March 1995)

197. Patrick Conway, *Currency Proliferation: The Monetary Legacy of the Soviet Union*. (June 1995)

198. Barry Eichengreen, *A More Perfect Union? The Logic of Economic Integration*. (June 1996)

199. Peter B. Kenen, ed., with John Arrowsmith, Paul De Grauwe, Charles A. E. Goodhart, Daniel Gros, Luigi Spaventa, and Niels Thygesen, *Making EMU Happen—Problems and Proposals: A Symposium*. (August 1996)

200. Peter B. Kenen, ed., with Lawrence H. Summers, William R. Cline, Barry Eichengreen, Richard Portes, Arminio Fraga, and Morris Goldstein, *From Halifax to Lyons: What Has Been Done about Crisis Management?* (October 1996)

PRINCETON STUDIES IN INTERNATIONAL FINANCE

58. John T. Cuddington, *Capital Flight: Estimates, Issues, and Explanations*. (December 1986)

59. Vincent P. Crawford, *International Lending, Long-Term Credit Relationships, and Dynamic Contract Theory*. (March 1987)

60. Thorvaldur Gylfason, *Credit Policy and Economic Activity in Developing Countries with IMF Stabilization Programs*. (August 1987)

61. Stephen A. Schuker, *American "Reparations" to Germany, 1919-33: Implications for the Third-World Debt Crisis*. (July 1988)

62. Steven B. Kamin, *Devaluation, External Balance, and Macroeconomic Performance: A Look at the Numbers*. (August 1988)

63. Jacob A. Frenkel and Assaf Razin, *Spending, Taxes, and Deficits: International-Intertemporal Approach*. (December 1988)

64. Jeffrey A. Frenkel, *Obstacles to International Macroeconomic Policy Coordination*. (December 1988)

65. Peter Hooper and Catherine L. Mann, *The Emergence and Persistence of the U.S. External Imbalance, 1980-87*. (October 1989)

66. Helmut Reisen, *Public Debt, External Competitiveness, and Fiscal Discipline in Developing Countries*. (November 1989)

67. Victor Argy, Warwick McKibbin, and Eric Siegloff, *Exchange-Rate Regimes for a Small Economy in a Multi-Country World*. (December 1989)

68. Mark Gersovitz and Christina H. Paxson, *The Economies of Africa and the Prices of Their Exports*. (October 1990)
69. Felipe Larraín and Andrés Velasco, *Can Swaps Solve the Debt Crisis? Lessons from the Chilean Experience*. (November 1990)
70. Kaushik Basu, *The International Debt Problem, Credit Rationing and Loan Pushing: Theory and Experience*. (October 1991)
71. Daniel Gros and Alfred Steinherr, *Economic Reform in the Soviet Union: Pas de Deux between Disintegration and Macroeconomic Destabilization*. (November 1991)
72. George M. von Furstenberg and Joseph P. Daniels, *Economic Summit Declarations, 1975-1989: Examining the Written Record of International Cooperation*. (February 1992)
73. Ishac Diwan and Dani Rodrik, *External Debt, Adjustment, and Burden Sharing: A Unified Framework*. (November 1992)
74. Barry Eichengreen, *Should the Maastricht Treaty Be Saved?* (December 1992)
75. Adam Klug, *The German Buybacks, 1932-1939: A Cure for Overhang?* (November 1993)
76. Tamim Bayoumi and Barry Eichengreen, *One Money or Many? Analyzing the Prospects for Monetary Unification in Various Parts of the World*. (September 1994)
77. Edward E. Leamer, *The Heckscher-Ohlin Model in Theory and Practice*. (February 1995)
78. Thorvaldur Gylfason, *The Macroeconomics of European Agriculture*. (May 1995)
79. Angus S. Deaton and Ronald I. Miller, *International Commodity Prices, Macroeconomic Performance, and Politics in Sub-Saharan Africa*. (December 1995)
80. Chander Kant, *Foreign Direct Investment and Capital Flight*. (April 1996)
81. Gian Maria Milesi-Ferretti and Assaf Razin, *Current-Account Sustainability*. (October 1996)

SPECIAL PAPERS IN INTERNATIONAL ECONOMICS

16. Elhanan Helpman, *Monopolistic Competition in Trade Theory*. (June 1990)
17. Richard Pomfret, *International Trade Policy with Imperfect Competition*. (August 1992)
18. Hali J. Edison, *The Effectiveness of Central-Bank Intervention: A Survey of the Literature After 1982*. (July 1993)
19. Sylvester W.C. Eijffinger and Jakob De Haan, *The Political Economy of Central-Bank Independence*. (May 1996)

REPRINTS IN INTERNATIONAL FINANCE

27. Peter B. Kenen, *Transitional Arrangements for Trade and Payments Among the CMEA Countries*; reprinted from *International Monetary Fund Staff Papers* 38 (2), 1991. (July 1991)
28. Peter B. Kenen, *Ways to Reform Exchange-Rate Arrangements*; reprinted from *Bretton Woods: Looking to the Future*, 1994. (November 1994)

The work of the International Finance Section is supported in part by the income of the Walker Foundation, established in memory of James Theodore Walker, Class of 1927. The offices of the Section, in Fisher Hall, were provided by a generous grant from Merrill Lynch & Company.

ISBN 0-88165-253-9
Recycled Paper